Communication
Miracles
for Couples

Communication
Miracles
for Couples

Easy and Effective Tools to Create More Love and Less Conflict

Jonathan Robinson, M.A., M.F.C.C.

CONARI PRESS
Berkeley, CA

ISBN: 1-57324-083-4
Cover Design: Suzanne Albertson
Cover Illustration: Jennie Oppenheimer
Book Design: Jennifer Brontsema

Library of Congress Cataloging-in-Publication Data
Robinson, Jonathan, 1959–
Communication miracles for couples: easy and effective tools to create more love
and less conflict / Jonathan Robinson.
p.   cm.
ISBN 1-57324-083-4 (trade paper)
1. Communication in marriage.   2. Interpersonal communication.
3. Man-woman relationships.   I. Title.
HQ734.R623   1997
646.7'8—dc21   97-7473

Printed in the United States of America on recycled paper.
2 4 6 8 10 9 7 5 3 1

What Is a Communication Miracle?

When couples come to me for psychotherapy, they are often at their wits end. It's not unusual for them to be screaming at each other while they sit in my office. Secretly, both people in the relationship are hoping I will act as an all powerful judge, and, after listening to the "evidence" against their partner, proclaim them to be totally innocent and their partner 100 percent guilty. I disappoint them. Instead, I tell them they're both doing things that are making intimacy impossible. I ask them if they would be willing to spend a short time trying a totally different but highly effective approach to relationship communication. I ask the same thing of you. You may not agree with everything I say in this book. That's okay. Test my methods in your own life. If you do, I think you'll see something quite amazing— these methods can create miracles in your relationship!

I have a unique job. I'm a psychotherapist who promises to help couples in three sessions or less. Therefore, I've focused on how to quickly turn things around for couples deeply mired in problems. Sound impossible? It isn't. All that's needed is the right theory about what really makes human beings tick and the right techniques to effectively bring out the best in yourself and others. I'm excited to present these ideas to you because I know they work. Unfortunately, I've seen that a lot of the information that exists about communication is not truly helpful. In my own life, I've seen that the ideas I was taught in college or read in books simply didn't work in the real world of relationships. Yet, the information in this book has withstood the most difficult test possible: It even works with people who are deeply hurt, enraged, and ready to give up all hope. No one needs a book on how to communicate when they feel good, loving, and peaceful. What we all need is a book on how to communicate effectively when we're fearful, frustrated, or want to punch someone in the nose! The theory and methods in this book are so simple, and yet so powerful they will even work in the most challenging real life situations.

Of course, you need not be deeply mired in problems to find these ideas and tools of great value to you. The same methods that can make a conflicted relationship peaceful can help make a good partnership become truly fantastic. Even if you've been happily married for many years, I'm confident these tools will help you create more intimacy than ever before. In addition, although this book is aimed at helping couples, you'll find these same ideas will also help you communicate more effectively with your boss, coworkers, children, family, and friends.

I often hear people complain that *they're* willing to communicate openly, but their partner is not. It is indeed easier to talk with a willing, cooperative partner—but not essential. You can use many of the methods in this book without your partner being aware of what you're doing. All they will likely notice is that you are blaming them less and are therefore safer to talk to. Yet, if your partner is the type who would be open to reading this book, by all means encourage him to do so. (Throughout this book, in each paragraph I alternate between using male and female pronouns such as "him" and "her" or "she" and "he" when referring to individuals.) Many of the ideas are easier to use when both partners are making an effort to practice them. It can even be a good idea to read a chapter out loud to your partner and *immediately* make use of the ideas presented.

It's a shame that in school we get to learn how to speak a foreign language and even how to "talk" to a computer—but fail to learn how to skillfully communicate in an intimate relationship. Recently, a friend of mine stated, "I only wish I could communicate with my wife the way I can with my computer!" I found his statement to be funny, but sad. I asked him, "Why do you feel more comfortable with your computer than your wife?" He responded, "Because I know how to make my computer understand me and do what I want it to. I guess I've never figured out how to do that with my wife."

This book will help you communicate in a way your partner understands and enjoys. Your confidence and intimacy will grow as you learn to successfully satisfy each other's needs. Since the skills you'll be gaining are best learned in a certain order, I've divided the book into three sections. In Part I, "Creating Intimacy," you'll learn how to give your partner what they most want from you. When you know how to give your partner exactly what they want, intimacy deepens and a lot of problems simply disappear all by themselves. Part II, "Avoiding Fights," informs you how to avoid pushing all the wrong "buttons" and provides you with specific methods to ensure you never need to argue again. Part III, "Solving Problems Without Bruising Egos," offers many practical ways to solve problems, create lasting love, and effectively change undesirable behavior. I suggest you read this book all the way through, then reread appropriate chapters as the need arises.

At the end of each chapter, I include a brief summary to help reinforce what you've learned, as well as a single specific practice I suggest you do with your partner. As when learning to speak a foreign language, learning new communication skills requires some study and repetition. Most of the exercises in this book are extremely simple and can be done in fewer than three minutes. Yet, mastering the exercises will transform the quality of your relationship. I wish I could literally grab you through these pages and convey to you how important it is to practice the exercises I suggest. In my work with couples, I've repeatedly seen how these simple practices create miraculous changes. When you're done reading this book, I want you to have more than just useful ideas—I want you to have new skills that will dramatically increase the amount of love you experience.

Words can be like magic spells. Say the wrong set of words and your partner can turn into an angry monster. Weave the right words together, and your partner can quickly become a loving prince or princess. As you master the magic of effective communication, you'll create more intimacy and harmony in your relationship. I wish you the best of success in your journey of love.

Creating Intimacy

Chapter One

What We Want (But Never Ask For)

No act of kindness, no matter how small, is ever wasted.
—Aesop

In order to get the most out of your car, it helps to know what it needs to operate effectively. You need to know what fuel and oil it uses, and how to get things fixed when it's not running right. The same is true for human beings. Luckily, at our core, all human beings are pretty much the same. We all want the three As: acknowledgment, appreciation, and acceptance. In fact, the three As are like high-octane gasoline that makes the human personality run. They are the essential ingredients that convey love from one person to another. Without them we become defensive and refuse to let anyone in. If you want to have a great relationship, you will first have to satisfy your partner's needs for acknowledgment, appreciation, and acceptance. And the more effectively you can help him feel loved, the more loving he will be toward you.

I've created a metaphor that I find helpful in explaining how the human personality works. I call it "the self-esteem bank account." I define self-esteem as the degree to which a person feels good about herself in any given moment. Let's say the average person has about ten "dollars" in her self-esteem bank account. When people have only two dollars in their bank account, they become violent. In newspapers, we read about people who went berserk when someone simply looked at them the wrong way. These people were at two "dollars" of self-esteem. When people are at zero "dollars" of self-esteem, they often try to kill themselves. With only ten "dollars" of self-esteem, we're highly motivated to not lose or spend any of our meager supply. Yet, the way we tend to go about protecting our account is almost always ineffective.

When couples are having difficulty, they inevitably blame their partner. Blame is a way of trying to "take" self-esteem "dollars" from your partner and give them to yourself. Unfortunately, this results in your partner feeling attacked, who then proceeds to blame and insult you in self defense: "You think *I'm* selfish, you should look in the mirror. You're the one who *everyone* thinks is selfish!" The cycle goes on. Have you ever been in one of these downward spirals? I sure have. It's no fun at all. Neither partner ends up getting the love and respect they really want.

Even if your partner is very upset, *the key to get him to be able to hear you is to give him plenty of acknowledgment, appreciation, and acceptance.* The three As are like deposits for your partner's self-esteem bank account. When you give your mate the three As, his self-esteem bank "balance" temporarily goes up. As his bank balance goes up, he will naturally become more loving, more giving, and better able to listen. Therefore, when your partner is feeling stressed, the best thing you can do is make a "deposit" into his self-esteem bank account. Almost like magic, he will become more agreeable toward you. As he is better able to listen to you with love, you'll feel better too. The destructive cycle will be over.

Bob and Jill came to see me for counseling as a last measure before filing for divorce. Bob and Jill were what I call "subtle blamers." They never shouted or called each other names, but the underlying intention was still to "score points" at their partner's expense. I explained to them the concept of the self-esteem bank account, but Jill would still make her subtle, blaming statements. Each time she did, I would stop her and ask, "Do you think Bob is more or less likely to listen to you after blaming him like that?" It soon became obvious to Jill why Bob "never listened" to her.

Jill asked me, "Well, how *can* I get Bob to hear me?" I told her that Bob will need at least some funds in his self-esteem bank account before he can risk listening to you. I suggested she first acknowledge or fully validate Bob's *experience* of her. Normally, when Bob told her his point of view or how he felt, Jill would say how wrong and ridiculous he was. This invalidation of Bob's feelings and reality just made him shut down more. So I asked Jill, "What's the *positive intention* behind Bob trying to explain his actions to you?" She responded, "He wants to show me how he's right and I'm always wrong." This statement made me aware Jill was lacking funds in her *own* self-esteem account, since she was feeling blamed. Therefore, I *acknowledged* and validated her experience. I said, "I understand you feel blamed by him and I bet that doesn't feel very good." Once I had acknowledged her experience, she was open to hearing what I had to say.

If, in the previous example, I had told Jill she was wrong about Bob's intention, she would not have been open to hearing me. It's a little-known fact that human beings are equipped with a secret device in their brain called a "blame detector." When anyone tries to blame us or make us wrong, even in the most subtle manner, our blame detector alarm is triggered. When our alarm goes off, it automatically shuts down the ability of our ears to hear whatever anyone says to us. Had I made Jill wrong for what she said, her ears would have shut down, and I would have been wasting my breath to say anything more. When people have low funds in their self-esteem account, they need to have their version of things be acknowledged *before* they can hear what *you* have to say. Acknowledging their view of things is not the same as agreeing with them—or suggesting they're right and you're wrong. It simply means you validate their personal experience. You accept that what they say is the truth *as they see it.*

Once I had acknowledged Jill's view of Bob, I repeated the question, "What do you think was Bob's *positive* intention of explaining his actions to you?" This time she said, "What do you mean by positive intention?" I explained that a person's positive intention is what they ultimately want from an action they take. Jill thought about it and finally said, "I guess he's explaining himself so I will stop blaming him and finally accept him as he is." Bingo! I told her that what everyone ultimately wants is to feel acknowledged, appreciated, and accepted, and the more you give these three things to your partner, the more they will give them to you.

I suggested to Jill that she first accept Bob's version of reality by validating his experience. She did this by stating, "I can see how you've felt blamed by me, and how that must have really hurt. I'm very sorry you've felt that way." Next, I suggested she communicate exactly what she *appreciates* about her husband when she's not upset with him. As Jill sincerely told Bob how important he is to her and described things he does that she treasures, he became less defensive. He began to get tears in his eyes. Then, Jill proceeded to tell Bob about the fear and hurt she'd been feeling because they haven't been getting along. Bob listened intently. As Jill finished talking, Bob tearfully reached over to hug his wife. They both apologized for the hurt they had caused each other. The downward spiral that had been going on for months ended in fewer than five minutes. A communication miracle.

Acknowledgment

People often ask me, "What's the difference between acknowledgment, appreciation, and acceptance?" I define acknowledgment as *being willing to agree that your partner really is having the experience they say they are having.* For example, let's say your partner says, "I'm sick and tired of you nagging at me." Perhaps you might respond, "I'm not nagging you, I'm simply telling you how to clean up properly." This seemingly innocent response would likely lead to a juicy disagreement. Why? Because it invalidates your partner's reality and feelings. From *their* eyes, you *are* nagging, and they are really bothered by it. Until you acknowledge their viewpoint and feelings, their ears will be turned off. By indicating you understand their perspective and their feelings, it allows them to be open to *your* perspective and your feelings.

In the preceding example, you might acknowledge your partner's words by saying, "I can see you're upset because you feel I'm nagging you. I guess that must really hurt. I'm really sorry you feel that way." Only when your partner feels fully acknowledged (understood) will they be open to hear your version of things, *not* before. Therefore, the *first* thing you should do when things get a bit heated on your mate's side is to acknowledge her experience—even if you think it's crazy. Remember, you don't have to agree with her perspective to acknowledge she has it. You might not have been nagging, but if she feels you have been nagging, that feeling will need to be acknowledged before she will be able to hear you.

Acknowledgment creates trust, and the more you validate her experience, the more she will trust you. Of course, the more you invalidate your partner's reality, the more she will feel she can't trust you.

I've created a simple way to remember how to acknowledge and validate your partner's experience. It's a fill-in-the-blank formula:

1. I see (or understand) you . . .
   Paraphrase what your partner's experience seems to be.

2. That must feel . . .
   Guess as to how such an experience must feel.

3. I'm sorry you feel . . .
   Guess as to what they're feeling.

Previously, Jill told me "Bob wants to show me how he's right and I'm always wrong." Rather than disagree with her, I used the acknowledgment formula. I said, "I understand you feel blamed by him, and I bet that doesn't feel very good. I'm really sorry you feel so hurt." That's all that was needed for her to feel I had really heard her. Now she was open to hearing me. As with all "fill-in-the-blank" methods, you need to adapt it in a way that uses your own words so it sounds sincere.

Unfortunately, most of us have had precious little experience in acknowledging our mate or having our own feelings validated by others. Instead of providing acknowledgment, most people immediately try to "fix" their partner when they express their pain—or defend against what they said if it seems like a blame statement. Neither approach works. When we're in pain, we *first* need our experience validated—before we can be interested in hearing ways to fix or solve the situation. That's just how human beings are. Yet, once your partner feels you've really heard him (by acknowledging his experience), he'll probably be very open to hearing whatever you'd like to say.

I often see clients get frustrated when they lovingly offer advice to their mate, only to see their partner knock down everything they say. It's not that the solutions being offered aren't effective; it's simply that the timing is off. People need plenty of sympathy before they are receptive to solutions. Have you ever had to deal with a three year old who's had her feelings badly hurt? If so, what did you do? You probably didn't start off telling her what she did wrong and what she should have done. Instead, my guess is you gave her plenty of empathy. To help the child know you cared, you probably said how sorry you were she got hurt. You lovingly listened to her tale of woe. Then, once all her tears were gone, if she seemed receptive, you may have offered some advice for how to better handle such a situation in the future.

When we're upset, we're just like three year olds. We need to know that someone understands how badly we feel. If instead of acknowledgment we are first given advice, we feel misunderstood. We feel cheated. Yet, once we feel our pain has been sufficiently validated, an opening for new input is created. Depending on your partner, he may need just a little sympathy and acknowledgment, or a whole lot. The more lovingly you offer your acknowledgment, the sooner he will be open to other things you'd like to say.

Appreciation

Appreciation is different than acknowledgment. I define appreciation as the art of telling your partner what you like about him or her. To get in touch with what you appreciate, you can simply ask yourself, "What do I like or appreciate about my partner?" By focusing on that question and occasionally expressing your answers to your sweetheart, it will help to keep her self-esteem bank balance in abundance. In addition, when difficulties arise between the two of you, expressing an appreciation can help your partner let go of blaming you or being defensive. After all, as her balance goes up, she will become more able to listen to you.

To make the best use of the art of appreciation, it's best to use it frequently. Just as it does little good to exercise infrequently, it does little good to appreciate your partner just once a month. The more you appreciate each other, the easier it becomes and the better you'll be at using this simple, but underutilized tool for creating intimacy. It's also helpful to make your appreciation very specific, precise, and graphic. It's not very effective to express a general appreciation such as "I like the fact that you're pleasant." On the other hand, it's very powerful to say, "I felt so proud of you when you offered to help that man in the wheelchair down those steps. You're always doing little things for me like buying me flowers or leaving me love notes. All those things really warm my heart." Can you sense how being specific and graphic is much more powerful? Let loose the poet in you to express your sincere appreciation to your partner.

Acceptance

Acceptance is the third A, and usually the last one to occur. Acceptance means you love your partner just as he is, warts and all. Another term for acceptance is "unconditional love." Acknowledgment and appreciation are both specific behaviors you can "do" with your partner, whereas acceptance is a shift in your attitude. In general, parents accept and love their infants even when they don't like their behavior. It's possible to have the same unconditional acceptance for your partner. In fact, your partner hungers for it.

I've noticed that many people are afraid to accept their partner unconditionally. They think that such a shift in attitude would lead to their partner walking all over them. Yet, the opposite is true. When people feel fully accepted, they do their *very best* to make their partners happy. After all, they are being supplied with the one food they are most hungry for. Of course, unconditionally accepting one's partner is not an easy thing to do. We tend to think we'll love someone more once they change in some manner. It's common to think, "If only my mate were nicer, thinner, richer, neater, and so on, *then* I would *really* accept him." The result of this way of being is that your partner never feels fully loved, and therefore never fully accepts you.

One way to help you accept your partner unconditionally is to learn to "tune into" the positive intention she has at any given moment. Since people all ultimately want to feel worthwhile and loved, they always have a positive intention behind their behavior. Even if your partner says things to hurt you, her positive intention is to increase the self-esteem in her own account—so she can feel worthwhile. You need not tell her you like her actions— because you don't. You need only be aware that, despite how she is acting, she does have a positive intention.

A practical way to help you feel acceptance for your partner is to simply ask yourself, "What is the positive intention behind what he (or she) is doing?" When you realize your partner is a human being in emotional pain, trying to get back to the feeling of love as best he knows how, you have the experience of acceptance. It's been said that everything people do is either a loving response or a cry for help. When babies cry for help, it's easy to see their vulnerability and their positive intention (to feel better). Therefore, it's easy to still love them, even if you don't like their behavior. When our partner "cries" for help by being a jerk in some way, it takes a conscious effort to see his positive intention and pain. Yet, if you look for it, it will surely be there. Accepting your partner does not mean that you never get annoyed at him. It merely means that you always love him—despite his occasional display of unskillful behavior. The attitude of acceptance is like a powerful medicine that heals the souls of both you and your partner.

Living from Abundance

Giving your partner the three As is not just something to do when you're upset at him or her. In fact, the more frequently and effectively you make your sweetheart feel acknowledged, appreciated, and accepted, the more loving she will be. She will "bank" the extra love you give, and thereby be better able to handle the small upsets that inevitably happen in the course of a relationship. As you give love more consistently to your partner, she will feel closer to you and give you her sincere appreciation in return. So begins the upward cycle to greater levels of love and intimacy.

It's amazing how well the three As work. With a couple named Shellie and Steve, Steve complained that his wife never wanted to have sex. Of course, Shellie's point of view was that Steve never wanted anything but sex! I suggested to Steve that he acknowledge (though not necessarily agree with) Shellie's point of view. He sincerely stated, "I understand you feel I'm always pressuring you to have sex. I bet that has felt very uncomfortable. I'm sorry that what I've been doing has made you feel that way." Shellie's body position, which was normally like armor, immediately softened. I suggested to Steve that he try to understand and accept Shellie's positive intention to feel safe and in control of her own body. Finally, I suggested to Steve that he begin to appreciate Shellie in nonsexual ways.

Steve was hesitant to begin appreciating his wife. He didn't have a lot of "dollars" in his self-esteem bank account, and he was afraid if he gave appreciation to his wife, he'd end up with even less. In a private session with Steve, I suggested he try a one-week "experiment" with his wife. For one week, he was to see what effect it would have to express his sincere appreciation for his wife both verbally and through warm, nonsexual hugs. Midway through the week Steve excitedly called me and said, "My wife has turned into a new woman! We've made love more times this week than in the entire previous year! What did you do to her?" I explained to Steve that learning to give your partner verbal appreciation and a caring touch can have unexpected benefits. When they walked into my office the following week, they looked like a couple on their honeymoon.

Try it for yourself. The next time your partner is in "one of her moods," acknowledge her reality, and then say what you appreciate about her. Perhaps you can give her a warm she expresses her pain. Such a simple gesture of acceptance can quickly transform how your partner feels. When you and your partner give each other acknowledgment, appreciation, and acceptance on a regular basis, you'll both feel like you're in heaven.

Miracle Reminders

1. When your partner is upset, make a deposit into his self-esteem bank account by acknowledging his perception of reality—even if you don't agree with it. Tell him you are sorry he is in pain. Then, communicate what you truly appreciate and respect about him.

2. Acceptance comes from recognizing your partner's positive intention and her pain. To tune into her positive intention, simply ask, "What positive feeling does she ultimately want from this behavior—even if she is trying to get it in an unskillful manner?" As you learn to accept your partner even when you don't like her behavior, you'll be giving your partner and yourself the gift of unconditional love.

3. By giving your mate (or anyone else for that matter) acknowledgment, appreciation, and acceptance instead of blame, you'll see a major change in how she listens and responds to you.

Mastery Practice

Try acknowledging and appreciating your partner this week. Validate her feelings and experience of the world if she feels bad by saying something like, "I understand you. . . . That must feel. . . . I'm really sorry you feel so bad." Find things to appreciate about your partner by asking yourself, "What do I like and/or appreciate about my partner?" When specific things occur to you, tell him. Notice what effect this has on your partner and on your relationship.

Chapter Two

Charming Your Partner's Heart

───────────

At the touch of love, everyone becomes a poet.
—Plato

I have a question for you: For $500 could you make your partner feel upset in less than one minute? Most people answer an emphatic "Yes!" To accomplish this, you would probably bring up some event, person, or question that invariably makes your partner irritated. We even have a term for this—"pushing my buttons." When someone pushes our buttons, it is commonly accepted we have no choice but to get upset. Over time, our partner usually learns where all our "buttons" are.

While "pushing my buttons" signifies a way our partner can easily make us upset, we have no phrase for the opposite effect—when our mate does something that invariably makes us feel loving. We could call it "pushing my love buttons," but there's no poetry in a phrase like that. I prefer to call it "charming my heart." When someone charms us, it's as if they have cast a spell of enchantment over our heart. A wonderful way to experience more love in your relationship is to learn automatic ways to charm your partner's heart. When your partner feels fully loved by you, guess how she'll treat you? Soon, you'll both be charming each other's heart in an upward spiral that leads all the way to heaven. Ahhh, how sweet it can be!

During the honeymoon stage of your relationship, you and your partner probably felt like you were swimming in a warm, sweet pool of tenderness. Why? Because you were not contending with any big problems yet, and you were expressing your love in many different ways. You wrote notes to each other, you bought little gifts, and you treated each other with the utmost kindness and caring. A wide-angle approach like that is bound to work. Of course, you can't keep expressing your love in all those same ways, year after year. If you're like most couples, you simply don't have the time to express love in all the ways that are possible. Yet, you still want to experience a lot of moments of tenderness. When you learn how to efficiently charm your partner's heart, you can create magical moments of love instantly, no matter where you are or how much time you have.

To know what makes your partner feel truly loved, it's necessary to realize each person has different rules or laws as to what true love is. Case in point: Many years ago I was with a girlfriend I'll call Cheryl. I was giving her a nice shoulder massage when she suddenly blurted out, "Would you cut that out!" Totally caught off guard, I said "Cut what out?" She annoyingly stated, "You're always massaging me. You're always touching me. Why do you have to be so grabby?" It was true—I frequently massaged her. So I said to her, "I do that to show you how much I care about you." She quickly responded, "Well, I don't *feel* very loved. After all, you never *tell* me you love me." She was right again; I never actually said the words "I love you" to her, although she frequently said them to me.

Cheryl and I had a long discussion about this episode, and we finally realized what had been going on. While I was growing up, whenever I was being spanked or punished, my parents would say, "We're doing this because we love you." Therefore, the words "I love you" had a negative connotation to me. I figured, talk is cheap. The way to *really* show someone you love them is to touch them in pleasant ways. That was my rule of how real love should be expressed. On the other hand, while Cheryl was growing up, she had an uncle who frequently gave her massages. One day, this uncle sexually molested her. Therefore, she took my massages as being a precursor of impending doom. We both thought we were expressing love to each other, when in fact we were unconsciously pushing each other's buttons!

The way we tend to express love to another person is, in most cases, the way in which we would like to receive it. I gave Cheryl massages because that's what makes me feel loved. Even if a gorilla gave me a massage, I'd feel totally loved. Cheryl frequently told me she loved me because that's what she wanted to hear. When people are unaware of their partner's preferred ways of feeling loved, they end up expending a lot of energy that goes unappreciated. Yet by knowing exactly what helps your partner feel safe and loved, it becomes infinitely easier to create intimacy on a consistent basis.

There is a simple exercise you can do with your partner to find out how best to "charm his heart." Have him become comfortable in a chair, and then say the following: "Close your eyes, take a deep breath, and begin to think of a specific time you felt really loved by me. Remember that time as clearly as you can. Remember where we were, what we were doing, and exactly what happened that let you know I really loved you." Give your partner a minute or so to fully reexperience such a moment. Then proceed. "What was most important in letting you know I fully loved you? Was it something I said, the way I looked at you, the way I touched you, or something else?"

Sometimes your partner will immediately know what it was but, if not, try saying the following: "Thinking back to this time you felt really loved by me, in order to know I fully loved you, was it necessary that I say something to you?" Wait for their response. Then continue, "In order to know I really loved you, was it critical that I looked at you a certain way?" Once again, wait for his response. Finally, ask if it was necessary that your sweetheart be touched in a particular way, or that you perform some action for him. Once you have a lead, continue to ask questions that are even more precise. For example, if your mate says, "It's the way you were talking to me," ask him, "What about the way I was talking to you helped you to feel loved? Was it the words I said or the way I said them or both?" Eventually, you will find a precise behavior that leads to charming his heart. If you desire, you can ask your partner to remember another time he felt totally loved by you. Although the exact same behavior may come up in this new scenario, you might find a whole new way of helping your mate feel fully loved by you.

I had a couple in my office named Sarah and Jim who both complained that they didn't feel loved by the other. I taught them about charming their partner's heart, but Jim was having a hard time doing it properly. Sarah's main way of feeling loved was through hearing the words, "Honey, I really love you," in a very soft and gentle voice. Every time Jim tried to say these words, they came out wrong. He sounded angry, frustrated, or apathetic. Finally, I took him into a different room, and I coached him till he said the words in just the right way. He walked back into my office, sat down, and said "Honey, I really love you," in a really sweet tone of voice—and Sarah immediately got tears in her eyes. Jim was so surprised at this result that he quickly turned to me and said, "Hey, this stuff really works!"

Actually performing the behaviors that charm your partner's heart may feel a bit weird to you. After all, it's probably not what would make you feel loved. Your partner may even feel loved doing the exact opposite of what would work for you! For example, when you're upset, you might want to talk about your feelings, while your partner may really want to be left alone. That's why it's critical to know what really makes your partner feel loved, and act accordingly—even if it feels strange to you. With practice, you'll get used to expressing love in the ways your partner prefers.

By knowing how your own heart is charmed, you can communicate this important information to your partner. Try the previous exercise on yourself, or have your partner read it to you. You may be surprised to discover exactly what your partner does that creates a warm feeling of safety and love in you. Once your mate knows how to efficiently help you feel loved, she can more easily and consistently show you she cares. Such behavior is like "money in the bank" of your self-esteem bank account.

My partner, Helena, and I have found the ability to charm each other's heart to be immensely helpful in our relationship. By performing the previous exercise, she learned that even my worst moods can quickly melt away when she gently massages me. I learned that saying the exact words, "I'm crazy about you," never fails to make her feel totally loved. And there are other things too. Watching "Star Trek" together or eating in a particular restaurant always makes her feel safe, loved, and appreciated. So we do those things often—and I get a lot of massages. And the more she charms my heart, the crazier I am about her. (She charms my heart a lot, so I'm now a complete lunatic about her.)

Every time you charm your partner's heart, you're making a "loving deposit" in to your *shared love* account. Your shared love account is like a bank balance you share together. When things are going well, there's a lot of love put into "savings." When both of you consistently make deposits in to your shared account, you feel abundantly in love. If the account goes to zero, your feelings for each other can become bankrupt. Dealing with problems is often like making a withdrawal from your shared love account. If the challenge is easily resolved, it's a small withdrawal. If the problem creates a big, messy, ugly scene, you can create the equivalent of a bounced check.

It's *much* easier to handle problems when there's an abundance of love in your love account. Therefore, make frequent deposits of love in your relationship account by charming your partner's heart. Remember to do the little actions that make a big difference in how your partner feels. It will immediately help both of you feel wonderfully intimate, and, when problems arise, you'll have plenty of love banked to help you ride out the storm.

Miracle Reminders

1. People have specific, simple things that can be done or said to them to make them immediately feel loved.

2. You can find out how to easily charm your partner's heart by requesting she remember times she felt fully loved and asking what specifically made her know you really loved her.

3. When couples consistently take the actions that charm each other's heart, it creates an abundance of love in their shared "love account," which makes it much easier to handle problems when they arise.

Mastery Practice

If you haven't already done so, find out what helps to charm your partner's heart. The shorthand way of doing this is by asking your partner, "When are a couple of times you've felt most loved by me?" Pause for his answer, then proceed. "What helped you know during those occasions that I really loved you?" Keep asking for as many details as possible. Also, ask yourself these questions and tell your partner what he does that helps you feel fully loved.

Chapter Three

Creating Love Beyond Words

There is only one happiness in life, to love and be loved.
—George Sand

Some of the most powerful ways to charm your partner's heart can be done without uttering a single word. Psychologists estimate that 93 percent of the impact of our communication occurs through nonverbal cues. That means the words we say only account for 7 percent of the meaning and impact of our communication! Most books on communication focus only on saying the right words, while ignoring how to use nonverbal methods for creating intimacy and safety. Fortunately, there's a science to being able to nonverbally create feelings of acceptance and appreciation with your partner. I have found the four methods outlined in this chapter to be particularly effective and easy to learn.

The Universal Language

The first technique for silently creating safety and love with your partner is to simply smile when you first see them. A warm smile tells your partner you're in a good mood, you appreciate her, and you're happy to see her. There's nothing you could say that would be as inviting as a simple smile. If you went up to your mate and said, "Hi, I just want you to know I'm in a friendly mood, and I fully accept and appreciate you," she would probably look at you like you were on drugs. Yet, a friendly smile is a silent way of saying just that. A warm smile gives her an immediate sense of acknowledgment, appreciation, and acceptance. It makes her feel fully at ease. Once such a warm tone is set, it makes it easier to move to deeper levels of trust and intimacy.

Smiling has more impact than most people can imagine. Studies have been done in which a smiley face was painted inside every cell in a large prison. Immediately, violence in the prison went down by more than 25 percent. Your partner subconsciously judges how much you care for her by watching for your nonverbal cues. If every time you see her, you put a judgmental look on your face, she will pick up on it, even if you don't say anything. The opposite is also true. If you smile and seem happy whenever you see your partner, she will feel very appreciated and accepted. Her self-esteem bank balance will temporarily rise, and she will immediately become more loving and available to you.

The human smile is the one universal expression that means basically the same thing in every culture. When human beings are happy and friendly, they smile. It's built into our biology. In fact, if you force yourself to smile, it will immediately improve your mood. It may seem strange, but a very effective "treatment" for depression is to simply wear a device that forces the corner of one's lips up! By holding this expression, pleasure releasing chemicals called endorphins are released into one's brain. So my advice is to get into the habit of smiling when you first see your sweetie. It will make both of you immediately feel good.

Mirroring

A second method for silently creating rapport with your partner is to "mirror" or mimic their body position. Often, when we feel connected with our partner, we unconsciously sit or stand the same way they do. It's a way of being similar to another person, and the more you're like someone else, the more they'll *tend* to like you. Some people worry that if they sit or stand like the person they're with it will be noticed and seem weird. It won't. People aren't aware of how their own body is, so if you sit like them, they won't notice it on the *conscious* level. But subconsciously, their brain will be saying, "This person is just like me— therefore I can trust them." Almost magically, they will feel there is something about you that makes them feel totally at ease. Without even saying a single word, they'll feel more intimate with you.

Many years ago, I had a dramatic experience of the connection that can come from this mirroring. Cheryl, my former girlfriend, had a father who was a military officer. At the time, I had a bohemian lifestyle living in spiritual communes, hitchhiking across the country, and so on. The information Cheryl's father had heard about me made him want to avoid me. Yet finally, Cheryl convinced her dad to meet me one time for dinner. He greeted me at the door with a frown on his face. His arms were tightly folded across his chest. He bellowed, "Well, Mr. Robinson, I've heard a lot about you!" I took the same body position, and, in a similar tone of voice bellowed back, "Well Mr. Smith, I've heard a lot about you too, sir!" Cheryl thought I had suddenly gone psychotic. She had never seen me stand or talk that way.

Throughout dinner, I mirrored Mr. Smith. Although he wanted to hate me, subconsciously his brain was telling him, "This boy is just like you." Although he didn't know why, by the middle of the dinner, he felt a mysterious rapport with me. Soon, he became more at ease, and, as he did, I resumed being my normal, mellow self. After dinner, when Mr. Smith briefly left the room, Cheryl took me aside and said, "What did you *do* to my dad?" I said, "What do you mean?" She responded, "While you were in the bathroom, he told me he thought you were the finest young man he had ever met!" As this story shows, matching someone's body language is an enormously powerful way to create feelings of trust and connection.

When mirroring your partner, it's not necessary that you imitate every little movement they make. All you need to do is stand or sit in basically the same way as him or her. If he's sitting in a very relaxed manner, sit that way yourself. If he's standing straight and formally, follow his lead. Mirroring happens all the time without people being aware of it. The next time you're having a really good conversation with your partner, notice how both of you are sitting or standing. You'll probably notice you're in roughly the same body position. By consciously matching the body position of your partner, you can *consistently* create feelings of acceptance and trust on a subconscious level.

The Treasure of Touch

A third tool for creating a love beyond words is to frequently touch your sweetheart in a caring, nonsexual manner. It is now commonly known among health professionals that babies need to be held during their first few months of life in order to survive. Without a certain amount of touch, even well-fed babies will die. Besides its physical importance to our well-being, touch is an important way we show our acceptance and love. Without this loving form of "soul food," it's easy for our self-esteem bank account to go bankrupt. Yet, in this culture, most of us are touch starved.

Touch was the first form of communication we understood as infants. Therefore, it can affect us in a much deeper way than mere words. As we become adults, we develop filters and defenses that help to protect us from being affected by words. Nowadays, we are bombarded by so many advertisements that we learn to diminish the impact of almost everything we hear. Yet, touch is different. We tend to think that a person's touch is very "honest," whereas their words are subject to question. A loving touch can slide past a person's defenses and touch them at their core. If you want to know how to powerfully and efficiently give your partner the three As, you need to learn how to touch your mate in a loving way.

A loving touch is completely different than a sexual touch. Some people confuse the two, and they end up paying a big price. Sexual touching is great, but it doesn't replace what a nonsexual touch can do. Many of my female clients complain that their partner never touches them unless they want to have sex. When this occurs, women typically interpret this behavior as the man saying, "I don't really like you, but I'm willing to have sex with you to satisfy my own selfish needs." It's no wonder that women in such situations are not aroused by their partner's touch. Yet, when men frequently touch their partners in a caring, nonsexual manner, the women feel safe and loved. When a woman feels truly safe and loved, she becomes much more interested in sex than when she feels she is being used.

It's not only women who need frequent and caring touch. Men also hunger for it. Of course, if a man isn't getting his sexual needs met, he'll likely interpret all touch from his partner as an invitation to make love. Yet, once a man's sexual needs are filled, there is nothing he'll appreciate more than a relaxing shoulder or neck massage.

Obviously, men and women are different when it comes to their sexual and touching needs. In a recent study, 70 percent of all women said they would gladly never have sexual intercourse again as long as they were able to cuddle or have a long hug each day with their partner. I advise my counseling clients to find out what their partner's precise touching needs are and to satisfy them as best they can. Although there are a few exceptions, the basic rule in relationships is the more you satisfy your partner's needs, the more they will want to satisfy your needs. I encourage couples to communicate about the precise forms of touch they most and least desire. We tend to assume that other people are like us, which just isn't true. As you and your partner regularly touch each other in enjoyable ways, the amount of intimacy in your relationship will skyrocket.

Laurie and Jeff came to my office complaining of a lack of passion in their relationship. They were both successful career people, highly intelligent, and very friendly with each other. They even communicated pretty well and were adept at avoiding blame or arguments. From the neck up, everything was in good working order, but from the neck down there was no energy. They would have sex about twice a month, but it lacked passion. They came to me wondering what, if anything, was wrong.

I asked them how much they touch each other throughout the day. They each gave me a look like, "What does *that* have to do with anything?" From the expressions on their faces, I knew I had hit pay dirt. Their minds were being massaged with nice words and good conversation, but their hearts, bodies, and souls were being ignored. I wrote out a "prescription" for them that said the following:

R/x: Give or receive three warm, caring touches a day other than at bedtime. The following "touch vitamins" are acceptable:

1. Vitamin H: Hugs lasting longer than ten seconds.

2. Vitamin M: Massages lasting longer than thirty seconds.

3. Vitamin F: Feathering (or lightly touching) your partner's hair and scalp area.

4. Vitamin C: Caressing any part of your partner's body for more than ten seconds.

They took the prescribed medicine. A week later they were physically all over each other in our counseling session, whereas before they had been on opposite sides of the couch. If I hadn't been there forcing them to be civilized, I think they would have made love right there in my office! Nonsexual touch on a regular basis can be strong love medicine.

Electric Sex

A fourth and final way to make love without words is to practice a method I call electric sex. Although it doesn't involve any sexual touching, electric sex can feel as intense as the most profound lovemaking. The instructions are simple: Sit facing your partner so you can comfortably hold both of their hands. Look into your partner's eyes, then breathe in unison. If the partners are heterosexual, it's best if the woman breathes normally while the man matches inhalations and exhalations. By noticing when the woman's shoulders gently rise and fall, it's possible to know when she begins to inhale and exhale. After a minute or two, you'll both get in the same rhythm, and it won't take any effort to breathe together. Continue looking into each other's eyes and breathing together for at least five minutes.

If an alien being asked you to describe exactly how a man has sex with a woman, it would not sound very interesting. The mechanics of sex sound downright strange. You might say, "The man inserts his penis into the woman, and, while in this position, they move their hips and pelvises back and forth for several minutes." Such a description hides the magical feelings and connection that can happen when a couple makes love. The same is true for electric sex. A simple description of its method doesn't do it justice. However, with the right background music and lighting to set a loving mood, electric sex can be a very profound experience. I hope you try it.

In workshops I lead, I have couples practice electric sex for ten minutes with each other while they're still in the workshop. A lot of them get hooked. It's one of the fastest ways to plunge into a very profound level of love. Of course, it's also one of the scariest. Since it works so well for some couples and not so well for others, I recommend you give it at least one sincere try. I know couples who excitedly tell me they both enjoy it a lot more than regular sex. Whether you like it or not, you'll find it to be powerful. It's an experience not to be missed.

Miracle Reminders

1. Most of the impact of what we communicate actually happens through nonverbal messages. By learning how to establish intimacy with your partner without words, you open up a whole new way to experience the love and connection you yearn for.

2. By smiling when you first see your partner and matching their body position, you can help your partner feel safe and appreciated by you. Such simple gestures work on a subconscious level, yet they can have very powerful effects.

3. Nonsexual touch and the electric sex experience are both ways to create an immediate and deep feeling of connection with your partner. The more effectively you satisfy your partner's touch needs, the more they will be open to satisfying your needs.

Mastery Practice

During the next few days, focus on using nonverbal methods to increase feelings of intimacy with your partner. Try smiling, mirroring your partner's body position, touching her frequently, and/or using the electric sex technique. Pick one of these methods right now and vow to use it tonight with your partner.

Avoiding Fights

Chapter Four

Would You Rather Be Right or Be Loved?

The strongest principle of growth lies in the human choice.
—George Eliot

I've got good news, and I've got bad news. The bad news is, if you want a happy and loving relationship, you're going to have to give something up: your insistence on being right. When you insist on being right, what you indirectly communicate to your partner is that she is wrong. You simply can't insist on being right (a form of blame) and have intimacy. Believe me, I've tried. It's like trying to have complete darkness and light in the same room. The good news is, if you're willing to let go of being right, you can easily experience plenty of love, harmony, and fulfillment in your relationship.

Conflict is inevitable between people. There is no getting around it. But conflict is not the problem. When handled effectively, difficulties can bring two people closer together. In fact, it would be nearly impossible for deeper intimacy to develop between partners without the aid of an occasional conflict. What really tears couples apart is blame. Blame, or the insistence on being right and making one's partner wrong, is like a slow-acting poison. It can gradually creep into the entire way couples talk to each other—until all the love once shared becomes completely polluted.

Since couples' problems stem largely from their need to be right, let's look at this phenomenon more closely. When in a blame mode, all you know is that you are being more than fair, while your partner is being totally unreasonable. In desperation, you present clear-cut evidence to show him just how wrong he really is. I guess we all secretly hope that one day, after stating our case, our mate will say something like the following: "Gee, I finally see what you've been trying to tell me! I've been totally wrong, and you've been right all along! I am so sorry I've hurt you. Could you please forgive me for the errors of my ways?" Have you ever had someone sincerely say that to you? Nor have I. Clearly, the blame game does not ultimately get us what we want.

There are many ways to have a good relationship, but there's only one thing going on in bad relationships—blame. Unfortunately, when we insist on being right, *everything* we say will come out wrong. Since blame *never* works, when you strongly feel you're right, the first thing you need to do is dramatically change *your* attitude. If you don't, your partner's blame detector will soon be triggered, and then you'll have a real mess on your hands.

How to Get Out of the Blame Mode

What can we do to communicate effectively when we're upset, frustrated, and certain we're right? Over the years, I've experimented with ways I can quickly get myself out of the blame mode and into a state of mind conducive to loving communication. After much trial and error, I finally came up with something that works for me and the many people I've taught it to. It's a series of three simple questions I ask myself when I think my partner is primarily to blame for whatever is going on in our relationship:

1. What is likely to happen if I insist on being right (and blaming my partner)?

2. Would I like to feel loved or be right?

3. What is something I especially like about my partner?

For small- and even medium-sized upsets, these three questions are very effective for changing how you feel. Once you *feel* differently, you can much more easily communicate in a way that leads back to intimacy. Let's look at each of these questions more closely. When you ask, "What is likely to happen if I insist on being right?" your mind should turn to think of the pain and failure you'll experience from being in the blaming mode. Depending on how you and your partner tend to handle such situations, you'll likely end up arguing with each other or giving each other the dreaded silent treatment. Neither feels very good.

Question number two asks, "Would I like to feel loved or be right?" This is not a trick question. In that moment, you may well prefer to be right. If that's the case, I would suggest you avoid saying *anything*—until you no longer feel that way. If you say anything, it will almost surely lead to an argument. Of course, it's okay to insist on being right and speak your mind. I still do that on occasion. But when I do, I'm not surprised by the miserable results I invariably have to endure.

If and when you're too angry to let go of being right, and just being silent with your anger doesn't feel like an option, there are a couple of things you can do. First, you can do what infants do—go have a temper tantrum. I'm serious. Young kids yell and beat the floor when they're really upset, and then after a couple of minutes of a tantrum, they're fine again. Once all the anger has been expressed, they feel good. Adults can achieve the same results by *going into a separate room* and beating the pillows on their bed for a couple of minutes. It feels good to let loose one's anger in a safe environment. By the time you're done, you'll feel more relaxed again and be able to communicate appropriately with your partner. If a tantrum on your bed isn't your style, in Chapter Five I have two more methods for effectively dealing with your feelings of anger, righteousness, and upset.

The one thing you must avoid is the one thing most couples do: They express anger and blame directly toward their partner. Admittedly, about one in a hundred people doesn't mind being yelled at. But the rest of us don't like it at all. It almost always leads to resentment, defensiveness, hurt, an escalation of the immediate problem you're dealing with, and a buildup of bad feelings that will create even more problems later on. I've seen couples who spend their entire relationship reacting to and recovering from their partner's anger. Like a bad Three Stooges movie, they spend most their time trying to inflict pain upon their mate—as a way of getting back at their partner for something she did to them. It's a sad sight to behold, and definitely a situation you want to avoid.

If you use the three questions before things get out of hand, you can tame the "blame monster" when it's small. If your feelings aren't so intense that you need to tantrum, and you realize you'd rather feel loved than be right, you're ready for the third question: "What is something I especially like about my partner?" Why ask such a question? Because your ability to communicate effectively with your partner is dependent on how you *feel* toward him or her. Even if you say the right words—but you're secretly blaming her, her blame detector will still be triggered (they can be darn sensitive), and her ears will completely turn off. On the other hand, if you dredge up some semblance of caring for your mate, she'll pick up on it, even if your words aren't just right. The easiest way to get back to feeling connected with your partner is to ask, and then do your best to answer the question, "What is something I especially like about my partner?"

For example, recently my partner, Helena, and I were scheduled to go to a business party in which I was going to be the speaker. Since Helena is frequently late for such things, I gave her several reminders as to when we had to leave. It didn't help. She was still not ready at the appointed time, and I was really upset. By the time we finally left, I was rushed, annoyed, and above all, absolutely right! I told her how upset I was, which simply served to trigger her blame detector and make her defensive. This just made me even more annoyed. Then, I remembered the three questions. Following I've listed the questions, along with the answers I thought of so you can better see how this method works:

1. What is likely to happen if I insist on being right and blaming my partner? *We'll probably have a tense and unpleasant silence for the entire drive to the party, and I'll continue to feel really annoyed and unsupported. Then, thanks to her* (I'm still in my blame mode), *I'll probably give a lousy speech and have a terrible time all evening.*

2. Would I like to feel loved or be right? *The biggest part of me would rather be right. After all, I am right. Yet, if I do that, I know I'm going to have a bad time, and I'll probably give a really bad speech. It seems it's important for all concerned that I at least try to get back to a place of love.*

3. What is something I especially like about my partner? *Let's see, there must be something about her that I can remember liking. I guess I kind of like how she gives me shoulder rubs whenever I need one. And I like how she smiles when she's in a good mood. And, of course, I like how she becomes really excited to see me when I've been away all day.* (I picture each of these scenarios in my mind for greater emotional impact.)

By this time, I feel a trickle of love penetrating my heart. As I continue driving, I reach my right hand over and place a single finger on her hand. She places a single finger on my finger, and our two fingers interlock. We both sit like this, silent. Neither of us wants to make the next move—since that would require letting go of being right. But after a minute or so, the desire to melt back into a place of love grabs both of us. Simultaneously, we take each other's hand warmly into our own. We smile, and the anger is gone. We look warmly into each other's eyes and giggle. Helena says she is sorry she was late. I say I'm sorry I got upset. As we continue our drive to the party, we're in love again. In fact, we're like newlyweds. At the party, we have a great time, and the speech goes really well.

It can be hard to remember what you like about your partner when he does something you resent. Therefore, before the next time you get angry at your mate, it is helpful to create a list of several things you really appreciate about them. In fact, try it right now. Think of specific times your sweetie did something that *really* touched you. Then, the next time you feel your partner is to blame for whatever is going on, you'll be able to remember something you appreciate about her. As you remember and picture these things, your mood will change. You'll soften. Your partner will notice and respond to your new mood by being more open to you.

I've created an acronym that can help you remember the three questions whenever you need them: WILL WISE. It can help to think that going from being upset to being loving takes an act of will, and that such an act will make you wise. Following, I've capitalized and/or underlined the key letters that lead to the acronym:

1. What Is Likely to happen if I insist on being right?

2. Would I Like to feel Loved or be right?

3. What Is Something I Especially like about my partner?

As you can see, the first two questions both use the acronym WILL, while the third question uses the acronym WISE. If, upon answering question number two you realize you would rather be right than feel love, again my advice is that you don't say anything. In this state of mind, anything you say can and will be used against you by your mate. Instead, use the methods for dealing with big upsets outlined in the next chapter or go into a separate room and have a tantrum (hitting your pillows). After you've had a tantrum, you may be ready to let go of your need to be right. Ask again, "Would I like to feel loved or be right?" By then, your answer may have changed. If it has, proceed to question three so you can emotionally connect with your partner.

In seminars I lead on communication, people often ask me, "But what do you do if your partner really is the one at fault? For example, what if an alcoholic man comes home drunk and beats up on his wife?" First of all, most real life situations are not this clear-cut. Yet, even in a situation like this, blame may seem like a reasonable response, but it's never truly useful for getting the results one wants. In this example, if the wife blames her husband for his behavior, he's likely to become even more violent or more drunk. But if she can sidestep the blame game and stay in a centered state of mind, she'll be more able to deal with the situation in a harmonious manner. She may well decide she needs to leave him because he's an alcoholic, or she may decide to call the police to protect herself. Yet, if she performs these actions without resorting to blaming him, she will more likely achieve a better result than if she insists on adding fuel to the fire.

Since the tendency to feel you're right and the other person is wrong is so strong, it's helpful to take a minute to really convince yourself that blame never works. Think back to times in the past in which you blamed a partner for something. Did insisting on being right ever help the situation—or did it just push your partner further away? How about when partners of your past blamed you? Did that ever make you feel more intimate and cooperative with them? If you're like most people, when you review blame's "track record," it's pretty easy to see that it always interferes with true intimacy.

You now have a practical method for helping get past the tendency to blame. But what if your partner starts blaming you? Showing your mate how she is wrong for blaming you is counterproductive, and it violates the principle you're suggesting she follow. As I mentioned in Chapter One, when your mate blames you, the best thing you can do is to acknowledge her experience—which is different than agreeing with her. The simple act of validating her experience may totally shift the energy in your interaction. Remember, your true goal is get your mate back on the same team as you. As long as either of you blame the other, you're acting as if you're on different teams. Yet, intimacy results from acting as if you both belong to the same team, and you both have the same goal—to feel loved and accepted. In later chapters, I'll provide additional ways to get back on the same team with your mate once blame has taken hold.

Letting go of the tendency to blame is not an easy thing to do. You will surely make mistakes. Yet, since blame never works, you can count on your partner to remind you when you're stuck on being right (you'll notice their blame detector has been triggered). If you notice your partner getting defensive or not hearing you, immediately ask yourself the three questions before you say another word. The three questions will help you change how you feel toward your partner. As your feelings change, you'll notice something amazing: Your mate can really hear you when you let go of your need to be right. And when your partner begins to really hear you, true intimacy can be restored.

Miracle Reminders

1. Intimacy requires that we let go of being right and let go of blaming our partner. When we blame our partner, their blame detector is triggered, and they can't hear anything we say.

2. To get out of the blame mode, ask yourself: What is likely to happen if I insist on being right? Would I like to feel loved or be right? What is something I especially like about my partner?

3. If you realize you'd rather blame your partner than feel love, go into a separate room and let out your anger. Then see if you're ready to proceed through the three questions. If not, use the methods for big upsets outlined in the next chapter.

Mastery Practice

The next time you see that you're slightly upset at your partner, ask yourself the three questions. Attempt to feel the answer to each question, as opposed to simply answering them on an intellectual level. When you answer these questions to yourself, notice if it helps you to avoid blaming your partner. Notice if it helps you to feel differently and/or communicate in a more loving manner.

Chapter Five

How to Never Argue Again

Look at a person's light, not their lampshade.
—Jerry Jampolsky

Why do couples argue? After all, we all know that arguing is definitely not an effective form of communication. Long ago, I figured if I knew the real reason why couples argue, I could create an antidote to arguing that would actually work. After many years of watching so-called lovers beat each other up with words, I've come up with a theory that explains why couples argue, and how they can avoid ever arguing again. The methods I've discovered to avoid arguments really do work! In fact, they work so well that, if you use them as I suggest in this chapter, you may never have another argument again.

Before divulging exactly how to sidestep all arguments, it's important to understand what causes arguments in the first place. Arguments begin when one or both partners dip below a certain level in their self-esteem "bank account." The reasons for the temporary dip in self-esteem can be anything—a bad day, a snide comment, or simply a lousy mood. Once a person feels bad, the first thing she tends to do is look for someone or something to blame. If you happen to be in the area at the time she feels bad, you make an easy target. If you're adding gasoline to the fire of her bad mood, so much the better for blaming you.

There's an old saying that "It takes two to have an argument." Quite true. When we're in a bad mood, the first thing we try to do is raise our level of self-esteem. Unfortunately, the way we do this is completely ineffective. Typically, we try to bring our partner down to our level, so that, *in comparison to our partner,* we no longer have a lower level of self-esteem than she has. We mistakenly think that bringing our partner down will, in effect, make us rise. That's why, when we're in a bad mood, we seem to want to pick a fight. Misery loves company. When we get below a certain level of mood or self-esteem, this babyish way of behaving takes over, and our unsuspecting mate almost always falls into our trap.

Once an argument has begun, we make another mistake. We think the way to feel better is to prove that we're right and our partner is wrong. I guess the logic is, if we're right and they're wrong, we'll gain valuable and much needed self-esteem points. Of course, it doesn't work like that. As we attack our partner, they fight back. Like wounded animals fighting for survival, we get vicious. We say things simply to hurt our partner, once again thinking that if we can wound them we'll at least be in a better position than they are. It can get pretty ugly.

For many years, I coached couples to gently express their needs without blame as a way of sidestepping arguments. In my office, under my watchful eye, it would work quite well. Yet, couples often reported it didn't work so well back at home. When in a nasty mood, they would invariably express themselves in a way that blamed their partner for their feelings. I finally understood why honest communication wasn't working. To communicate honestly, it's necessary to be a sane, rational person. Well, when we're in a really bad mood or in the heat of an argument, we become temporarily wacko! We behave like bratty babies, and babies are not very verbally adept. I finally realized that honestly expressing one's needs and feelings was not going to be the Holy Grail that would end all arguments.

When I noticed we behave like bratty babies when we get into a fight, I asked myself, "What helps bratty babies feel better?" The answer was obvious: They like to be held. As parents gently hold their baby, the baby soon feels better. Before you know it, the infant is giggling and happy. I wondered if a similar approach might work with adults. After much trial and error, I found something that works even better than I expected. I call it the "Spoon Tune."

One of the great things about the Spoon Tune is how easy it is. When we're upset, we don't have the capacity to do anything complicated. Luckily, the Spoon Tune has just two simple steps to it. First, at the earliest sign of upset, lie down with your partner in the spoon position. Spooning is a way in which many couples sleep. It consists of having one person's front side hugging the other person's back side. Couples can also spoon standing up if they're in a place where they can't lie down. Although holding your partner in this manner is probably the last thing you want to do when upset, force yourself to do it. Sometimes I think to myself, I have a choice between spooning for four minutes and feeling fine, or I can stay upset and ruin the rest of the day. When I clearly see that those are my two options, I begin spooning.

Next, while in spooning position, breathe in unison with your mate. Generally, it's best for the bigger partner to follow the breath of the smaller partner. When the smaller person inhales, the other partner should inhale. When the smaller partner exhales, the other should exhale. Hold each other and breathe in unison like this for at least four minutes. Don't say anything. As soon as your mind wanders, focus once again on breathing in unison with your partner.

No matter how upset you are at the beginning of this simple exercise, you will find yourself quickly calming down. The combination of being in the spooning position and breathing together puts people back on the same wavelength. When you share energy in this way, it creates a feeling of safety and connection at a very deep level. Although your mind may be racing and storming, your bodies and souls can't help but connect. By the end of four or five minutes, you may not even remember what you were upset about. At the very least, you'll feel more connected and safe, and you'll be much better able to work things out without hurting each other.

One of the first times I used this method with Helena, I was extremely upset. After all, I knew I was totally right, and she was being totally unreasonable (isn't that always how it feels?). Previously, we had made an agreement that if either of us asks for "a tuning," we must do it—whether we want to or not. Well, I didn't want to Spoon Tune, because I was just about to show her how wrong she really was! But our agreement was that if one of us doesn't agree to spoon within two minutes of being asked, he or she has to rip up a $10 bill. Just the thought of ripping up a $10 bill sobered me up, so I proceeded to grudgingly Spoon Tune with her. I was determined to keep being upset throughout the four required minutes—so I could then finish telling her how wrong she was. It didn't happen that way. Below is a transcript of the thoughts inside my head as I began to Spoon Tune:

I can't believe she's making me do this. She is being such a bitch! She won't even listen to me because she knows I'm right.

(We breathe together.)

I'm not going to simply let go of this. After this spooning is over, I'm really going to let her know how unfair she's being.

(We breathe together.)

Well, I may have contributed a bit to the problem, but it's mostly her fault. After all, she's the one who started it.

(We breathe together.)

Well, she probably didn't mean to hurt me . . .

(We breathe together.)

Perhaps I was also a bit insensitive.

(We breathe together.)

It wasn't really that big of a deal.

(We breathe together.)

Gee, I sure enjoy holding her.

(We breathe together.)

What we share together is really very special. I'm grateful this isn't a major problem.

(We breathe together.)

Four minutes are up. Helena asks me, "Was there something you wanted to say to me that you didn't get a chance to say?" I respond, "Umm, ahh, I don't really remember what we were upset about. I feel good again, and that's all that matters." And that's really how it felt. Once the feeling of connection and safety is reestablished through the Spoon Tune, there is no need or desire to argue. You feel like you and your partner are on the same team again. If there is still an issue to resolve, it's much easier to do so. Oftentimes, the issue, which seemed so big just minutes before, has become totally unimportant.

I have found a couple of things helpful in using the Spoon Tune effectively. First, it's important to create an agreement with your partner that the next time either of you ask to spoon, the other partner will immediately proceed to do so. It's useful for this agreement to be iron clad, preferably in writing. When you're upset, spooning with your partner is not the first thing you'll want to do. Therefore, you might want to create a penalty for failing to keep this agreement. Helena and I have agreed to rip up $10 if one of us refuses to spoon within two minutes of being asked. In six years, we've had to do this only once. Some couples I know have agreed to buy their partner a special gift if they refuse to spoon. Whatever you both agree to is fine, as long as it helps to motivate both of you to keep your commitment.

Once you begin the Spoon Tune, no talking is allowed. If possible, find a place to lie down together. If that's not possible, spoon standing up. The key to doing this method successfully is to breathe together. As you breathe together, try to focus on and be present with your breath. Use your breath as a meditation. By focusing on your breath as it goes in and out in rhythm with your partner's breath, you will feel more peaceful, safe, and connected. Spoon for at least four or five minutes.

Once you're done spooning, you have a couple of options. You can simply forget about whatever led to the upset and go about your business, or, if you feel it's necessary, you can talk things over with your partner. If you need to work something out, you'll be in a much better frame of mind to do so. You can proceed to nimbly use the methods for working through problems that are discussed later in this book.

You need not wait until you're upset to use the Spoon Tune. In fact, it's a great way to connect with your partner anytime. Many couples find it to be an easy and satisfying way to unwind after a stressful day. It can also be a very effective way to connect with your partner before making love. The hardest thing about this method is remembering to use it. Be on the lookout for times when you or your partner begin to get upset or either of you feels stressed. In order to use the Spoon Tune correctly the first time you get angry with each other, it's a good idea to try a practice run when you're not upset. By having your partner read this chapter and create an agreement with you about using this method, you'll be fully prepared to sidestep your next argument. Once you use it the first time and see how well it works, you'll be hooked.

And What Else?

I have found one other method useful in circumventing arguments. It works by helping to create a safe space for communicating the negative feelings that often lead to arguments. I call the method "And What Else?" Like the Spoon Tune, the key to its success is its simplicity. It's almost impossible to misuse. It's especially useful for couples in which one partner feels a strong need to talk, instead of being touched, when they are upset.

"And What Else?" works by allowing you to speak without the threat of any interruptions. While you speak, your partner is not allowed to say anything in response to what you say, except for the words "And What Else?" Meanwhile, your job is to explore and verbalize all that's going on with you. When and if you take a break in your speaking, your partner will encourage you to go on by simply saying, "And what else?" When you feel you've said absolutely everything you want to say, you declare, "I'm done." Then, if your partner desires, she can request that she speak while you listen. Below is a transcript of a couple named Jenny and Joe performing this exercise:

> Jenny: Can we do "And What Else?"
> Joe: Okay.
> Jenny: I feel like you don't appreciate anything I do anymore, and I'm getting sick and tired of catering to your every need! I feel like you treat me like a maid.

Joe: And what else?

Jenny: You expect me to do the dishes, the laundry, and take care of the kids without even saying a thank you, and yet the moment I ask you to do anything, you give me a dirty look. Why should I even try? It's not worth it.

Joe: And what else?

Jenny: I'm tired. I'm really tired. I need to know you appreciate me. I want to feel special. I want you to treat me like I'm more important to you than a baseball game. I want to feel close to you again.

Joe: And what else?

Jenny: I want you to hug me more. I need to be held. Remember how you used to hold me and tell me funny stories? I miss sharing those moments with you. I want us to share special moments again. I don't want to nag you or blame you. I just want us to care more about each other. I know I've been upset at you lately. I guess I just need to know you still care about me.

Joe: And what else?

Jenny: I'm done.

Jenny starts out attacking Joe, but as she's allowed to explore all that's going on with her, she softens. She begins to realize what she's really needing, and she acknowledges the part she's played in the problems they're having. Had Joe started disagreeing with each thing she said, an argument would have surely ensued. But instead, Joe's soft response of asking "And what else?" provided Jenny with a safe environment to go beyond her blame.

In the martial art of aikido, students learn to not resist the energy of their attackers. Rather than try to defeat their attackers, aikido masters simply aim to render their opponent harmless. A similar philosophy underlies "And What Else?" By not resisting the feelings and thoughts of your mate, you make it impossible for him to maintain an adversarial position toward you. This allows him to go beyond his anger and into the deeper causes of his discomfort. Anger and blame are like the skin of an onion; peel off the skin and there are other layers of emotion that exist underneath. If you create a safe environment for your partner to explore what's beneath his anger, he will often do so.

Another advantage of "And What Else?" is that it can help the listening partner to really hear what the other person is saying. Normally, when someone is angry or hurt, she gets defensive and fails to fully understand her partner's perspective. As he speaks, it's common to begin rehearsing a rebuttal to his accusations. Yet, if you know you aren't allowed to respond other than to say, "And what else?" the momentum to rehearse your response diminishes. As you listen better, your partner will feel more accepted. As he feels more accepted, he will feel safe enough to go beyond his blame and defensiveness.

Just as you did with the Spoon Tune, it's important to make some sort of agreement with your partner regarding when you'd be willing to use the "And What Else?" method. For my counseling clients, I suggest they both agree to use it within five minutes of being asked to do so, unless one of them has a prior commitment—such as an appointment with a third party. As soon as one person has said all he wants to say, the other partner can ask for her turn to be listened to if she desires.

It's best that partners delay discussing what was said during this exercise—for at least a few hours. That way, you can avoid responding from emotional upset. If your partner says something you feel you need to respond to, wait until you feel more centered. Trust me on this one. If you try to clarify what your partner said or immediately respond to them in any manner, it will likely lead to an argument. You may even have good intentions for asking them a question or making a clarifying remark—yet it will still likely lead to a fight. The inability to immediately respond is what really makes this method useful. Don't try to compromise the method. I suggest you wait at least an hour before you respond to anything your mate says during the "And What Else?" process.

Arguments occur when two people are talking (or yelling), and no one is listening. This is a clear sign that communication has broken down. In the heat of such exchanges, a lot of hurtful and destructive things can be said that can damage the level of trust you share with each other. If you make an agreement with your partner to use either or both of the tools I've discussed in this chapter, I'm confident you will experience a positive shift in your relationship. When two people go beyond the tendency to argue, they can open themselves to a deeper level of trust, safety, and love.

"And What Else?" like the Spoon Tune, can be used anytime. You need not wait until you or your partner are upset. Some couples use it as a ritualized way to unwind after coming home from work. Having someone attentively listen to you can be a very healing experience. In a matter of a few minutes, you can let go of the past and feel fully refreshed and acknowledged. Play with these valuable communication tools. They can be like stairs that allow you to climb to higher levels of love in your relationship.

Miracle Reminders

1. Arguments are typically caused by one or both partners having a temporarily low supply of self-esteem, which results in blaming one's partner, as an ineffective way of trying to elevate one's own self-esteem. When a person is in such a state, it is not useful to try to discuss something.

2. By holding your partner in the spooning position and breathing together for four or five minutes, it will calm you down if you're upset or stressed. Agree to do this with your partner the next time either of you get upset. The Spoon Tune is also a great way to relax and bond with your sweetheart when you want to be more intimate without talking.

3. When your partner is upset, you can gently ask her, "And what else?" during pauses in her speaking as a way to encourage her to let off steam. As your partner is allowed to vent without any interruptions or defensive replies, she will usually calm down and become more centered.

Mastery Practice

The next time you begin an argument with your partner, immediately ask him to do a Spoon Tune with you. See how differently you feel after four or five minutes of tuning with him. Or if you prefer, you can do the "And What Else?" game instead. Right now, make an agreement with your partner to use one of these tools the next time either of you request it. You might even create a negative consequence if the tool isn't immediately utilized when requested. It's a good idea to put this agreement in writing.

Chapter Six

Speaking Your Vulnerable Truth

Beyond all appearances of separation, we are one with the Heart of Love.
—Joan Borysenko

We all long for magical moments in which we feel deeply connected to our partner. Unfortunately, it's also what we avoid in a hundred different ways. Yet, the directions for getting back to an experience of intimacy can be found within the word itself: in to me see. When we let ourselves be vulnerable with our partner and show her how we feel and what we want, the level of intimacy we experience rises. On the other hand, when we hide our true feelings and desires, and instead resort to blame or intellectualization, intimacy disappears.

After years of watching couples communicate, I've seen most couples don't know what I mean when I say communicate in a soft, vulnerable manner. It's as if it's a foreign language they haven't been exposed to. Therefore, I teach a method that helps people to speak this unusual "dialect." I call it "I feel/I want." This method simply reminds people to communicate what they're feeling and wanting. By saying these two things, we allow our partner to see into who we really are at any given moment. Such intimacy can be scary. Before you even attempt such an exercise, it helps if you have already established a level of trust with your partner from using the ideas and methods in the first several chapters.

Marcia and David were in my office struggling to use the "I feel/I want" method. I asked David to express how he feels when Marcia slams the door when they've been arguing. He said, "I feel she has a problem, and I want her to stop getting upset like that." I replied, "But how do you feel?" After thinking about it for a bit David stated, "I feel angry that she has a problem." While this statement was a little bit better, it was still a subtle form of blame. I've noticed that even the smallest amount of blame makes it impossible for partners to hear each other. No matter what you say once your partner's alarm has been triggered, she can't hear you. In fact, the *more* you try to get her to hear you, the greater her walls go up.

Once I repeatedly saw how subtle forms of blame would "slip" into the "I feel/I want" tool, I made it more precise and structured. I now have couples use the following format:

1. When you (briefly describe situation), I feel (sad, hurt, afraid, or impatient) because I (explain the psychological need you have that leads to feeling the way you do).

2. What I want is (describe the precise action you would like your partner to perform).

I suggest when you express how you feel to your partner that you use only the four emotions listed: sad, hurt, afraid, or impatient. But what if you feel angry, frustrated, enraged, or devastated? My suggestion is to translate those feelings into one of the four suggested feelings. Why? Because when your partner hears you say words such as angry, frustrated, or devastated, it will usually trigger his blame detector. And once his ears fall off, no communication is possible. I've found the word *impatient* can almost always substitute for the feeling of frustration. Likewise, *hurt* works well for devastation, and beneath all anger is really feelings of hurt and/or fear. By saying you feel sad, hurt, afraid, or impatient, you can let your partner basically know how you feel without triggering his blame detector!

After you express what you feel, avoid placing the blame for how you feel squarely in your partner's lap. To say, "I feel hurt because you are insensitive," will certainly start the alarm sirens wailing. That's why you should say the words *because I* after you state how you feel. Then, explain *which psychological need* causes you to feel bad in this situation. For example, you might state, "When you watch TV when you come home after work, *I feel* hurt *because* I have a need for you to hug me when you first come home." Even if your partner does something terrible, stick with talking about yourself, rather than blaming her. This will help your mate to hear your pain, rather than immediately get defensive and completely block out what you say.

In a later session with Marcia and David, it came out that David had previously had an affair. Marcia first blurted out, "I feel outraged that you could be so cold-hearted!" Of course, David immediately got defensive and a whole lot of bickering and accusations came flying out. Eventually, I coached Marcia to say, *"I feel* deeply hurt and afraid *because* I love you a lot, and I'm afraid to lose you." David really *heard* that. Tears welled up in his eyes as he said, "I am so sorry I hurt you. I'm here because I love you—so we can work through this. I don't ever want to leave you." Then David and Marcia hugged as if they had just been saved from a burning building.

When your partner gets defensive, it simply means you triggered his blame detector. Take his defensiveness as a sign you need to try again to communicate without blame. The *more* you stick to the structure I've outlined in expressing your feelings, the more likely it will work. The reason this tool is difficult to use is because it doesn't give the feeling of immediate satisfaction that comes from blaming your partner. On the other hand, it ultimately gets you what you want, whereas blame does not.

Following I've listed four statements a client of mine said to her partner. Each statement triggered her husband's blame sirens in a big way. Under each of her unsuccessful attempts to communicate, I've written how I suggested she speak to her husband. Notice the different energy that comes from her initial blaming statements and from the translated communication:

1. "I feel totally unsupported in this relationship."
Translation: "When you don't talk to me all evening, *I feel* really hurt and sad *because* I need to know you care about me."

2. "I am fed up with having to clean up after the messes you make."
Translation: "When you leave dishes in the sink, *I feel* hurt *because* I need to know you respect me, and I interpret your not doing your dishes as a sign you don't appreciate me."

3. "All you care about is your own sexual needs. You never even *think* about my needs."
Translation: "When you rush through foreplay, *I feel* hurt and impatient *because* I want to be able to share sexual pleasure with you, and I haven't had enough experience of doing that lately."

4. "I'm sick and tired of you watching football all day."
Translation: "When you watch a lot of football, *I feel* sad and afraid *because* I want to share more moments of fun and adventure with you, but I feel like I can't compete with an exciting football game."

Once you clearly express how you feel, your next job is to express what you want—without triggering your partner's ever so sensitive alarm system. Remember, he may have only a few "dollars" of self-esteem in his bank account, and if you say the wrong thing he will immediately get defensive or angry. You must proceed with extreme caution—as if making your way past an alarm system that can be set off by the slightest error. Most couples make the mistake of being far too general when they say what they want from their partner. If you say, "I want you to be more affectionate," it's likely to be met with defensiveness. This statement is far too general, which your partner would interpret as a major withdrawal from his self-esteem bank account. After all, he probably feels he is affectionate, and your remark implies he is wrong. Instead, you could say, "I want you to hug me when you first come home." This statement is precise, doable, and gives him a clear idea of exactly what you're asking for.

Following you will find four examples of what a client of mine said to his wife in an attempt to ask for what he wanted. Each of his statements triggered defensiveness in his wife. After a bit of coaching, he made his statements more precise. Once again, I've included "translated" statements to help you get the hang of how to do this.

1. "I want you to stop getting so upset all the time."

Translation: "I want you to take a walk around the block when you want to raise your voice or feel really angry at me."

2. "I want to have more passion in our love life."
Translation: "I want to try to make love using some methods from a book on tantric sex I've been reading."

3. "Stop nagging me to take you on an expensive vacation."
Translation: "I want you to understand why I worry about our finances, and from that understanding, help me plan a vacation that will fit within our budget."

4. "I don't want to go to any more parties with you because you're always flirting."
Translation: "When we go to parties together, I want you to limit yourself to just one drink and talk to Fred only when I'm around."

The more specific your communication, the easier it will be for your partner to satisfy your request and refrain from defensiveness. It's a win-win situation for both of you. However, in order for you to be able to speak this way you'll need to pause before you express what you normally would say. The way we normally speak is with blame and generalizations. To speak without blame and in a precise manner, you'll have to translate things in your head—or better yet, on a piece of paper. If possible, I suggest you write down exactly what you would say off the top of your head. Then, translate those statements into the "I feel . . . because I . . ." and ". . . what I want is . . ." format, making sure you stay specific and avoid all blame. It takes an extra effort to do this, but in the long run it will save you many hours of bickering.

The "I feel/I want" method will work in even the most hostile situations, such as when your partner is righteously upset at you. Not long ago, I told Helena I signed us up to take a class on the uses of pepper. She, being an avid cook, was quite excited. What I had failed to mention was that the class was really about how to use pepper spray for self-defense. Furthermore, the class was scheduled at a gun shop, and Helena hates anything having to do with violence or guns. When we met downtown, I realized I hadn't told her what the class was really about, and I knew she'd be upset. In addition, I had already plunked down $75 for the class, and it was starting in four minutes. Within those four minutes, I knew I'd face her anger for misleading her about the class. I also knew that taking a class in a gun store was the last thing on earth she would want to do. I was in trouble, so I pulled out my magical artillery, the "I feel/I want" tool.

As we stood at the entrance of the gun shop, I said to my sweetheart, "Honey, I feel afraid because I want you to do a big favor for me, and it's hard for me to ask you to do that when I think you might be upset with me. I forgot to tell you the class on pepper I signed us up for is really a class on how to use pepper spray for self-defense purposes. I am very sorry I forgot to tell you before now and that I misled you. I understand you don't like gun shops or thinking about violence. Yet, I feel so much love for you that I can't bear the thought of anything happening to you. What I most want is for you to do a favor for me by taking this class. I know it is not something you want to do, but it would mean a lot to me and would help me feel less anxious when you go on long hikes alone. Would you be willing to do this for me?"

Helena's face went from being very upset at realizing she'd been mislead to very soft as I told her why I wanted her to take this class. As if by magic, she instantly forgave me for misleading her and walked into the gun shop and took the class. It was a good thing she did. The following week, while hiking alone in a nearby forest, she was abruptly approached by a naked man. Since she had her pepper spray at her side, he didn't try to do anything. The proper use of "I feel/I want" can have positive consequences beyond what you might imagine and can turn almost any communication situation around in just a few moments.

Although the "I feel/I want" method sounds simple, it can take a while to master. The first few times you use it, you'll probably trip your partner's blame detector. You'll likely say you feel "really angry" or some other emotion that makes your partner's ears fall off. Allow yourself to make a few mistakes. If your partner tries to use the "I feel/I want" method with you, allow him or her to also make mistakes. Just like learning a foreign language, it takes time before it becomes second nature. The good news is the very first time either of you use this method correctly, you'll notice how effectively it works. While it may feel confining at first, I suggest you stick to the exact structure and emotions I suggested earlier. It will greatly increase the likelihood of your partner really hearing you. When you think about it, being able to use a few simple words to reliably create feelings of intimacy is downright miraculous. Of course, all magicians know the key to mastering their art is to practice.

Miracle Reminders

1. Intimacy develops from being vulnerable with your partner and by clearly expressing what you feel and what you want.

2. To avoid blame from slipping in, use the formula: When you (briefly describe situation), *I feel* (sad, hurt, afraid, or impatient) *because I* (explain the psychological need you have that leads to feeling the way you do).

3. The more precisely you describe what you want from your partner, the more likely she will be able to give it to you, and the less likely you will trigger her "blame detector."

Mastery Practice

Think of something that feels off or bad in your relationship that you haven't communicated to your partner. See if you can communicate it using the "I feel . . . because I . . ." and ". . . what I want is . . ." formula outlined in this chapter. See if you can avoid triggering your partner's blame detector as you communicate your feelings and desires. Notice how you feel after communicating this information to your sweetheart.

Chapter Seven

The Best Way to Create Lasting Harmony

Blessed are the peace-makers: for they shall be called the children of God.
—The Bible, Matthew 5:9

There used to be certain culturally defined rules about how to handle most of the challenges couples face. Men made the money to pay the bills; women did the housework and took care of the children; divorce was not an option. In the last thirty years, all the standards on which relationships lived in the past have broken down. With the breakdown of rigid rules, more equality and freedom of choice is possible. But, there's a price. Nowadays, it seems like there is less security and harmony than ever before. Rules, or agreed upon ways of doing things, help to create harmony by making it clear how to handle touchy situations. Since our cultural rules have broken down, a couple seeking harmony in the modern age must learn how to create and negotiate their own rules.

In his bestselling book, *Men Are from Mars, Women Are from Venus,* John Gray talks about the many differences between men and women. With great clarity, he shows how men and women have different ways of coping with upsets, resolving issues, and finding fulfillment in relationships. In essence, his powerful message is that men and women have different rules and expectations as to the proper way to do things. Yet, the truth is slightly more complex. In my counseling work, I've seen that it's increasingly difficult to generalize that "all women" and "all men" are a certain way. The reality is that each person has a unique set of rules about how to deal successfully with the myriad situations of modern-day life.

Tony Robbins, the author of *Awaken the Giant Within,* defines rules as the beliefs or standards a person has about what is needed in order to feel or experience something. For example, how much sex do you need to be satisfied? For some people, their standard is once a month; for others, it's twice a day. Those are very different rules. Unfortunately, when two people get together, they each bring literally hundreds of expectations about how things should be. To make matters worse, most couples fail to talk about their unique set of rules, because they assume that everyone has the same standards as they do. By effectively communicating our rules to our partner and learning about her unique expectations toward us, we can help create long-term harmony in our relationship.

In any intimate relationship, your partner will eventually violate many of your rules. When our rules are stepped on, we get upset. In fact, every upset in a relationship is due to two people having different ideas of the acceptable way to do things. When our rule is not respected by our partner, we feel hurt or rejected. We think that our standards are the right ones, while his way of doing things is wrong. Blame sets in. In my work with couples, I attempt to show them there are no universal standards of what should happen in a relationship. Is it right to have sex once a day, once a week, or once a year? Ultimately, it's really just a matter of personal preference. Once partners can see there's no clear-cut correct way of doing things, it becomes easier for them to share their needs without making their partner wrong for how they've acted in the past.

In Chapter Two, I discussed how to discover the rules for having your partner feel you really love them. I pointed out that, unless we specifically ask, we tend to assume what works for us will work for our partner. The same is true for any of the myriad ways we interact with one another. Each of us have very specific, unspoken ideas of how things should be. When you're upset, you might think your partner "should" warmly hold you and say nice things to you. However, your partner may be the type of person who thinks an upset person should be left alone to sort things out. Couples with such differing rules can drive each other crazy unless they bring their rules out into the open.

In general, I have found there are a dozen areas in which differing rules can lead to messy disagreements. A disagreement simply means that each partner has different rules for what's right, and they've never worked out an equitable solution. I call these areas of potential disagreement the "dynamite dozen" because if you don't discuss them, they tend to blow up in your face:

The Dynamite Dozen

(Areas in which differing rules cause considerable problems):

1. How to make money decisions; who is in control of money.
2. How often to have sex and other issues of sex such as birth control, what happens if the woman becomes pregnant, and so on.
3. How to treat your partner when she is upset.
4. How to show your partner your affection and love.
5. How to discipline the kids; what are the different responsibilities each parent has toward the kids.
6. What makes the relationship truly successful.
7. What is the proper way to listen to your partner; how much listening is necessary.
8. How to handle problems and major decisions that affect both partners.

9. How much quality time should be spent together each day or week.

10. How much TV watching is allowed.

11. How much alcohol and/or drug use is allowed.

12. What is the proper way to ask your partner to do things for you.

These twelve areas tend to be where rule disagreements have the most impact on a relationship. If you can come to agreement about how to handle these twelve issues, then you're likely to experience a lot of harmony in your relationship. However, if you and your mate have widely different rules on these issues and you fail to resolve them, you'll have a consistent source of tension in your relationship. Before you can resolve differences in your rules, you first have to know precisely what rules you and your mate have in these twelve areas. The way to find out your own rules is simple: Ask yourself, *"What does it take or what has to happen in order for me to feel good about (fill in appropriate subject matter from the dynamite dozen)?"*

For example, to find out your rules about sex, you'd ask "What does it take or what has to happen in order for me to feel good about the amount of sex we're having?" The answer that occurs to you is your sexual standard. If you want to find out what it takes to have a successful relationship (question number six), you'd ask "What does it take in order for me to feel I'm having a successful relationship?" Obviously, for some of these questions, you may have several rules. You may even have ten specific things that have to happen in order for you to feel you're having a successful relationship. That's helpful to know and extremely important to communicate to your partner.

Sometimes couples considering marriage come to see me, just to make sure there are no major problems they've overlooked. One couple, Jim and Janice, managed to avoid what would have likely been a "marriage from hell" by coming to see me. As is typical in such counseling sessions, I asked each of them their rules for the dynamite dozen. Very quickly, bombs were blasting away. In reaction to Jim's statements, Janice would exclaim things like, "You think it's okay to drink six beers *a day!?*" Or Jim would yelp, "You want me to spend five nights *a week* having quality time with you!?" It went on and on. Having met only two months before, they were still in the infatuation stage of their relationship. In one hour, we managed to put an end to that. They put their wedding plans on hold, and, after a month of trying in vain to negotiate compromises on their differences, they parted as friends. Despite the fact they broke up, I considered it to be a major success.

When asking your partner about her rules for the dynamite dozen, follow the same format as when asking yourself. Tell her you'd like to work out differences in how you do things before they mushroom into major problems. For each of the dozen issues, ask your partner, "What does it take, or specifically what has to happen, in order for you to feel good about (fill in the appropriate area)?" Try to get her to be as specific as possible. People have very precise rules, but they will sometimes fail to communicate them in a specific manner for fear you'll laugh at them. Therefore, create an atmosphere of trust and acceptance, and gently encourage your partner to reveal her intimate needs and desires. You may want to use the "And What Else?" method to create a safe environment that avoids any immediate comments on her perspective. In addition, to encourage your partner to share this information, it may be helpful for you to *first* share your own answers to each of these questions.

An easy way to state your rules to your partner is to fill in the following statement: "In order for me to feel good about our relationship, you need to do X (or X has to happen)." For example, to state your expectations in relation TV use, you would say, "In order for me to feel good about the amount of TV you watch, you need to watch less than ten hours a week and less than two hours in a single night." As you discover areas where you and your partner have different rules—and most likely you will—don't despair. If major differences exist, please refer to Chapter Ten in which I discuss a practical way to negotiate compromises that will allow each of you to feel loved and respected. For now, however, you just need to both feel comfortable enough to express your truth.

I've noticed people have great resistance to sharing their rules with their partner. Perhaps we like to live in denial and simply hope it'll magically work out without our effort.

Or perhaps we don't want to know there are real differences in our needs and desires. Whatever the reason, failing to share your rules is like walking into a valley full of land mines. You don't have to share your precise standards all at once, but if you notice that a certain area repeatedly gives you and your partner problems, discuss the rules you both have in that area. Listen to your partner without resorting to blame. Listen to your own rules and ask, "Are these expectations appropriate?" Since we picked up most of our rules from our parents, you may be dragging along standards and expectations that don't work for you anymore. If that's the case, consciously decide on new standards or rules that are more likely to work in your relationship.

In my own case, I used to have a rule that went something like, "If you love me, then you'll never get angry at me." I discovered this rule when stating what I thought was the appropriate way for my partner to deal with being upset. My rule stated, "In order for me to feel good about how my partner handles upsets, she would never express anger directly at me." Upon hearing myself say this, I realized it was a bit extreme. After all, what are the chances of having a partner who never expresses anger? Once I saw this as an unreasonable standard, I decided to change my rule to "If you're upset, then you should be willing to talk to me about it within two hours of the time you get upset." It used to drive me crazy when Helena got angry at me—since my rules didn't allow for any anger. Now, as long as she's willing to talk about it within a couple of hours, I feel okay.

When rules are openly discussed between partners, the level of blame in a relationship will often go way down. This is because the sharing of rules leads to greater understanding, and understanding is one of the best antidotes to blame. Once each of you have shared your rules, you may feel worse off than before because now you're aware of many more potential problem areas. Yet, rules that are openly expressed can be handled through negotiation and compromise (see Chapter Ten). It's the invisible expectations and standards that cause repeated problems in relationships. You'll experience deeper levels of trust, love, and security with your mate as you learn to share your rules and create agreements that work for both of you.

Miracle Reminders

1. Rules are beliefs about what needs to happen in order for you to feel a certain way. When your rules differ from those of your partner, problems occur until you can work out a mutually satisfactory agreement.

2. To disclose your own rules or to find out your partner's rules, ask "What does it take, or specifically what has to happen in order for me (or you) to feel good about (fill in the appropriate area)?"

3. Whenever you and your mate repeatedly have tension or problems about a certain aspect of your relationship, find out what each of you wants or needs in this area to feel satisfied. The dynamite dozen represents areas in which differing rules can lead to major problems unless some resolution is reached through negotiation.

Mastery Practice

What is a problem area that repeatedly comes up in your relationship? If nothing comes to mind, look through the dynamite dozen and choose one area that has given you and your partner trouble in the past. Use question number two to find out what are your mate's and your own specific expectations in this area. Try to get as specific as you can.

Solving Problems
Without Bruising Egos

Chapter Eight

How to Get Your Partner to Really Hear You

When you come right down to it, how many people speak the same language
even when they speak the same language?
—Russell Hoban

I'm waiting for the day when a couple tells me, "Jonathan, we really understand and listen to each other very well. That's why we're here and on the verge of divorce." It hasn't happened yet. The most common complaint I hear in my office is, "My partner doesn't really listen to me." People yearn to be heard and understood. It makes them feel acknowledged, appreciated, and accepted. Yet, most people think it's their partner's lack of listening that's the problem, instead of their *own* lack of *speaking* skills. No matter how poor a listener you think your partner is, it's possible to speak to him in a way that practically guarantees he will understand you.

Before discussing how to get your partner to understand you and your feelings, let's look at how to teach your partner not to hear you. If you were a scientist trying to train your partner to never fully hear you, this is what would be most effective: First, you'd begin by nagging your partner about unimportant issues. Then, when he didn't respond, you'd repeat what you said—only louder. Your partner would then be conditioned to believe that *everything* you said, even with a loud voice, was unimportant. Your increasing dissatisfaction with his behavior would show him that nothing good ever comes from your mouth and that tuning you out is justifiable.

Unfortunately, this approach to training a person to ignore you is exactly what happens to many couples. Luckily, there are remedies to this condition. As you practice these new ways of speaking, you'll find your partner's listening skills seem to miraculously improve. The first method for speaking so you'll be better understood involves learning to speak in metaphors.

The Magic of Metaphors

Metaphors are simple phrases that help us understand an experience or situation by linking it to something we already are familiar with. For example, when someone says "My relationship is like a battlefield," it helps us to quickly and graphically understand what their relationship is like. By using metaphors to describe your experience to your partner, you help him or her to understand you—both intellectually and emotionally.

Ron came to see me because he felt that everyone, including his wife, Margaret, didn't understand him. After ten minutes of hearing his complaints, I noticed I was becoming bored and started to tune him out. As he spoke in a monotone about how no one gave him any respect, I found myself unable to hold back a much-needed yawn. Not exactly good timing. I decided to teach him the magic of metaphors.

The first thing I asked Ron was, "What do you want your wife to understand about you?" Ten minutes later I still hadn't received an answer to my question—and I was doing more yawning than listening. So I asked a different question: "In a *single sentence*, what do you want your wife to understand about you?" He thought about it for a moment and said, "I want her to understand that her criticism really hurts and that I need her encouragement." With a sense of relief, I said "Great! Here's what you do: Think of a time your wife felt badly hurt in her life—possibly due to being criticized or rejected in some manner. Then, think of a time she got some form of positive feedback that really made a big difference to her. Perhaps it was a promotion or a surprise party or a really nice gift of some kind."

Ron took a minute to come up with the information I requested. He told me that Margaret's first husband, Paul, left her for another woman, and upon walking out the door said, "I don't think you could ever love a man." That hurt. Even after many years, she still remembered her former husband's parting words to her. On the positive side, Ron remembered how his wife reacted to an unexpected gift he bought her. She was visibly happy for weeks. With this information in hand, I suggested Ron tell his wife the following:

"Honey, when you criticize me it makes me feel like how you felt when Paul criticized you right before he left you. It hurts me that much and makes me feel hopeless. What I would like is more of your encouragement. In fact, when you say positive things to me, it feels like the time I bought you that necklace you love. It makes me *want* to succeed. Just like what happened with the necklace, it gives me a sense of pride and confidence."

When Ron expressed these words to his wife, he was amazed at the response. His wife got teary-eyed when she realized how much she had been hurting him. She immediately began encouraging him and even bought him a beautiful new suit he had been wanting. Ron was so surprised at the results achieved by this new way of speaking that he thought I had secretly called his wife and told her how to react! Yet, as he practiced "metaphor magic" with other people in his life, he realized no trick was needed on my part.

In order to practice this method, I've created a simple way to create metaphors that will help you be better heard and more clearly understood:

1. Decide what you're feeling. (The most common negative feelings are anger, hurt, sadness, fear, guilt, and frustration.)

2. Ask "When has my partner ever felt something like what I'm feeling and felt it with similar intensity?"

3. Make a list and decide on the best choice.

4. Say to your partner, "When (briefly describe your situation) happens, it feels like the experience you had when (briefly mention the corresponding situation he had)."

As always, do your best to translate my formula into your own words. You might find it helpful to write down exactly what you plan to say to your partner before you actually say it.

In the previous formula, I showed how you can create a metaphor to help your partner understand your feelings. However, to be fully understood it's important that your mate also understand what you *want*. Following is a four-step formula for creating metaphors to tell your partner what you *desire:*

1. Decide, in a single sentence, what specific behavior you want from your partner.

2. Ask yourself, "When has my partner ever wanted something similar and with similar intensity?" Or "When has my partner ever received something similar that had a big affect on him?"

3. Write down several examples and decide on the best one.

4. Say, "When you do (the specific behavior you want), it makes me feel like you felt when (describe your partner's powerful experience). My hope is that you will do it more often, because it has such a positive affect on me."

More Metaphors

If you're with a relatively new partner, you may not know enough of their history to create a metaphor based on their experience. In such cases, you can simply create generic metaphors. Generic metaphors are phrases that almost everyone can understand. The example I used about the relationship being like a battlefield is a good example. A person does not need to be a veteran in order to comprehend the dynamics of such a relationship. You can create metaphors for almost any experience or desire you want to communicate. All you need to do is compare one thing to another. Following, I've listed a dozen metaphors you might find helpful to use, but feel free to create your own as the need arises.

Metaphors to Express Negative Feelings:

1. When you do X, it makes me feel like a small child who's been abandoned by her mommy, not knowing if she'll ever return.

2. When you do X, it makes me feel like someone just spray painted obscenities all over my house.

3. When you say X, it feels like I've been kicked in the groin.

4. When you X, I feel like a baby who's being screamed at and spanked by a drunken parent.

5. When X happens, I feel like a maniac's got a gun to my head, and I don't know if they're going to shoot.

6. When you do X, it makes me feel like I've walked in totally naked to a formal dinner party.

Metaphors to Express Positive Feelings:

1. When you say X to me, it feels like Ed McMahon just knocked on my door and told me I won a million dollars.

2. When you do X, it feels like I'm being caressed and sung to by a choir of angels.

3. When you do X, it feels like all the people I love have gathered together to give me a surprise birthday party.

4. When X happens, it feels like seeing our baby for the first time.

5. When you massage my shoulders, it feels like a bus is being lifted off me, and I can fly.

6. When you smile and hug me when I come home from work, it's like being given a beautiful bouquet of roses.

You've probably noticed that many of these metaphors seem rather dramatic. In this day and age of TV and action-packed movies, you need to be dramatic for people to fully hear you. After all, you're literally competing with sixty channels of TV for your partner's attention! By using metaphors when you speak, you'll be training your partner to listen to you with more empathy and interest. And, as they say, half the battle of good communication is being heard.

You've Got It

I'm always asking other counselors for their best techniques for helping couples. My friend Barbara Reiner-Yaffee offered me this next technique, and I've found it to be quite helpful in having couples effectively hear each other. It's called "You've Got It." The instructions are simple. When you *really* want to make sure your partner hears you accurately, ask him or her if they'd be willing to play the "You've Got It" game. If they say no, then you *know* it's not a good time to say something important—try again at another time. But, if they agree to play, proceed to say whatever it is you want to communicate. Be as thorough as possible.

Make sure you include what you feel and what you want. Once you're finished speaking, ask your partner "What did you hear me say?" His job is to simply express back to you, *in his own words,* his understanding of what you said.

If you have ever played "Telephone" as a kid, you know "You've Got It" is more challenging than it initially sounds. If you remember, in "Telephone," someone whispers a story to a friend, who then proceeds to pass it on to someone else. By the time the last person says the story out loud for everyone to hear, it often has no resemblance to the original tale. To prevent such fabrications in "You've Got It," there is a single simple rule: The game isn't over until you feel your partner has accurately heard and understood what you said. When she convinces you she understood what you said, you excitedly state, "You've got it!" Then, take a break to congratulate yourselves—you deserve it.

The way this game typically goes in real life is not unlike "Telephone." It's helpful to keep your sense of humor close at hand. Be sure not to interrupt your partner as he feeds back what he thinks you said—even when he makes errors. Simply wait for him to finish and say, "You didn't quite get it." Then proceed to repeat the part you feel he didn't say or understand accurately. Continue this dialogue with your partner until you can truthfully say, "You've got it!"

For your amusement and information, I've included an edited transcript of a couple playing this game in my office:

Mary: I've been feeling like we never spend any quality time together anymore. You're either watching TV or doing some work project. We don't even watch TV together. It's like we pass each other in the night. Even on weekends, we seem busy all the time. You're either taking Scottie to Little League or going fishing with him. Where's the time for us?

Ralph: You feel I'm too busy, and I'm spending too much time with Scottie. You'd like for me to do more stuff with you—such as go to a movie or watch TV together.

Mary: (trying not to laugh) That's not quite it. I think it's great you and Scottie are doing things together; that's wonderful. It's just that I miss sharing special time alone with you.

Ralph: You want to have more alone time with me—maybe get a baby-sitter for Scottie and have fun on the town.

Mary: That's not quite it. I don't want *more* activities; I want to have quiet time alone with you. I want more intimacy and sharing.

Ralph: I hear you'd like to spend some quality time each week just talking, without any distractions, in an intimate setting. You want to share more special moments together, and you find it frustrating when that doesn't happen.

Mary: Honey, you've got it!

Ralph: Good, I'm going to go out and play poker with some buddies. You want to come? (Just kidding.)

A couple of precautions. First, don't play this game if you're angry. If you're angry, you might never say "You've got it." If you're really upset, turn to Chapter Five and use those methods instead. Second, don't play this game for every little thing you want to communicate. Your partner will resent it if you do. Rather, use it for truly important communications or when other attempts at being understood just aren't working. As an emergency method of being heard and understood, the "You've Got It" game is hard to beat.

Your Listening Investment

Another metaphor I've found useful in helping couples is that of a "listening investment." What is an investment? It's something you give time and/or money to, in hopes it will pay off profitably in the future. When you invest your attention in listening fully and with empathy to your partner, it usually creates dividends in the future. Your partner secretly keeps score as to how much and how well you've listened to her and, in most cases, will give you roughly the same amount in return. Listening is a way that helps your partner feel acknowledged, and can it be one of the most giving things you can do for the person you love.

We've talked about how to help your partner to hear and understand you, but how can you better understand and listen to your partner? After all, he probably doesn't speak in metaphors. Perhaps, on occasion, he's downright boring or confusing to listen to. However poorly he communicates, somehow you need to demonstrate that you respect and understand him—or you won't have any "dollars" in your listening account.

Couples sometimes become cheap in their willingness to invest in listening to their partner. This can create the experience of two people talking and no one listening. More commonly, it leads to the problem of partners who constantly interrupt each other. When you interrupt, what you're saying to the other person on a nonverbal level is: *"What you have to say is so predictable and such a waste of time that it's not worth my waiting a few seconds, and what I have to say is so important that, in order to not waste my precious time, I'm going to cut you off."* If you remember you really are giving your partner this message every time you interrupt, it will motivate you to avoid interrupting in the future. When partners interrupt each other in my office, I quickly stop them and have them repeat after me: "What you have to say is so predictable and such a waste of time that it's not worth my waiting a few seconds, and what I have to say is so important that, in order to not waste my precious time, I'm going to cut you off." After a few times of saying that, they realize how negative a message they convey when they interrupt their mate.

In addition to interrupting each other, I have found the most common mistake people make is immediately invalidating what their partner says. For example, if your partner says, "It seems like we never have fun anymore," how would you respond? Often, our first reaction is to get defensive and show how that's not true, but such a response would surely make your partner feel he's not really being listened to. In Chapter One I talked about the importance of acknowledging your partner's reality, even if you don't agree with it. But, to be a superior listener, you need to take one more step. You need to ask questions that help you *fully* understand your partner's perspective and feelings. When your partner says something that sounds untrue or outlandish to you, instead of getting angry or defensive, get *curious*. Try to find the details of *how* he has created his view of reality. I have found the following four questions to be particularly useful in understanding other people's feelings and point of view:

1. How do you feel about (the situation at hand)?

2. Why do you feel that way?

3. What leads you to think (whatever it is they seem to think)?

4. Can I do anything to help you to feel better?

When asking these questions, it's important to refrain from saying them in an accusatory manner. You're simply trying to better understand your mate's point of view. If your partner answers these questions in a blaming way, first acknowledge their pain. Seek to understand—instead of trying to justify yourself.

After I ask my clients these questions, I generally feel like I really understand what's going on with them. More importantly, they *feel* like I understand them. As I listen to their responses, I usually say nothing other than, "Uh huh, I see." Inside my head I might be thinking they are totally crazy to react in such a manner, but I don't say that out loud. In fact, when people feel they are really understood, they can usually let go of their negative feelings and return to a state of harmony and love.

Not long ago, I was seeing a new client whom I knew nothing about. Before she arrived, I sat down to meditate for awhile. By the time my client, Julie, arrived I was having a very hard time focusing on the outside world. Julie sat down and began describing to me some complex problem she was having, which involved several people. My mind was not able to follow her story whatsoever. Whenever I realized I had not heard what she said, I tried asking her one of the questions listed previously at what seemed like appropriate times. She would answer and move forward with her story, but I was already too far behind to make any sense of what she was saying. Therefore, all I could do was listen quietly and nod sympathetically to her problem—whatever it was about.

Although I'm usually more focused when counseling, my lack of focus in this session helped me learn a valuable lesson. Because I couldn't intellectually follow her story, I wasn't able to give Julie any instruction or advice. Mostly I just listened. At the end of the session, with tears in her eyes Julie stated, "Oh you've been so helpful! You really helped point me in the right direction. I am so grateful to you." I never learned what her problem was, but evidently it got solved. For a long time she referred other people to me. Asking people simple questions, and then listening intently can be one of the most loving things you can do for anyone. Being heard is healing, and the more you invest in hearing your partner, the more likely she will take the time to fully listen to you.

Miracle Reminders

1. Use metaphors that relate to your partner's life to grab his attention and help him understand what you feel and want. Create these metaphors by asking yourself, "When has my partner ever felt something like what I'm feeling (or wanting)?" Then say, "When (describe situation) happens, it feels like the experience you had when (briefly mention corresponding situation they had)."

2. To make sure your sweetheart understands you, you can play the "You've Got It" game. In this game, your partner feeds back in her own words what you're trying to communicate. When you feel she understands everything you said, you say, "You've Got It!"

3. The more you listen to your partner, the more likely your mate will listen to you. Draw out your partner by asking questions such as: "How do you feel about (the situation at hand)?" "Why do you feel that way?" "What leads you to think (whatever it is they seem to think)?" "Can I do anything to help you to feel better?"

Mastery Practice

See if you can create a metaphor that helps your partner understand how you feel about something in your life or relationship. Once you've created it, say it and see if she seems to better understand you.

Chapter Nine

How to Get Your Partner to Really Change

*My favorite enemy, the one most easily influenced for the better
is the British Empire. But my most formidable opponent is a man named
Mohandas K. Gandhi. With him I seem to have very little influence.*
—Mohandas K. Gandhi

People don't like to change. Change is hard. Change is work. As you most likely know from broken New Year's resolutions, even a change you want to make is difficult. So imagine how another person feels when you request her to change something about herself. Asking your mate to change implies she is flawed—something no one's ego wants to admit. Therefore, if you want your partner to change a particular behavior that bothers you, you need to be careful how you handle such a delicate operation. If you handle it perfectly, your partner will respond to your request and do her best to adapt to your needs. But one false move (or statement), and she'll dig in her heels and stay the way she has always been.

Since no one likes to change, I suggest you avoid asking your partner to do so unless something really bothers you. If you're always asking her to be different than she would normally be, eventually she'll simply tune you out or leave. So before asking your partner to change, ask *yourself,* "Is there any way *I* can adapt or change so my partner's behavior doesn't bother me so much?" Try to feel the resistance you have to that question. Your partner will manifest at least the same amount of resistance to being asked to change, so don't even ask her unless you've exhausted other possibilities.

There are three primary ways to get your partner to change. First, you can force him to change by threatening him or nagging him until he finally gives in. With this approach, even if he gives you what you want, his underlying resentment will make it a shallow victory. The second approach is to accept him just as he is, hoping his undesirable behavior will simply disappear if you love him unconditionally. Sometimes this works, and sometimes it doesn't. The main problem with this approach is that it can take the patience of a saint to love a person who does something destructive or annoying. In addition, your partner may not even understand what you'd like for him to change, which makes it unlikely he will do so no matter how loving you are. The third method for getting your partner to change is to speak in a way that sidesteps your partner's blame detector. The precise technique for doing that is what this chapter is about.

Getting your partner to change is analogous to trying to remove a tumor through surgery. When a surgeon performs an operation, she proceeds through a very precise and well thought-out plan. She carefully prepares the patient for surgery, gives an anesthetic to dull or eliminate the pain, quickly removes the tumor, and then helps the patient to recover. In the same way, you'll want to take your "patient" (your partner) through a similar four-step procedure. Although such a careful strategy may seem unnecessary, asking your partner to change, like surgery, can be dangerous business.

Getting Ready

The first step in preparing your partner for surgery—I mean constructive feedback—is to give him plenty of acknowledgment, appreciation, and acceptance. For your partner to change, he will first need to know you love him. Assuming you've established a degree of trust and safety in your relationship, the next ingredient you need is the right timing. Check to see how he is doing. If it's been a rough day, or you see he's in a bad mood, choose another time. When your partner's self-esteem level is low, no matter how careful you are, you're likely to trigger his blame detector.

If your partner seems to be doing okay, proceed to say something you appreciate about him. A sincere and heartfelt appreciation will temporarily raise his self-esteem "bank balance." Yet, I warn you: Don't offer appreciation only as a precursor of negative feedback. If you do, your partner will soon catch on. Hopefully, you're in the habit of appreciating your partner. If that's the case, one more positive comment will not immediately arouse suspicion. With an appreciation, you've prepared the patient for surgery. Now, administer the anesthesia. When telling your partner what you'd like him to change, communicating your positive intention is the best anesthetic. If you remember from Chapter One, your positive intention is the ultimate purpose or reason you have for giving your partner this feedback. For example, your positive intention might sound something like the following:

"Honey, I have a favor to ask of you. The reason I'm asking is because I really value our relationship. I think we're very lucky to share the love we have, and I want to make sure we can continue to strengthen our love in the future." That's it. Stating your positive intention helps to provide your partner with a favorable *context* for requesting he change. It softens the blow of saying something that ordinarily would trigger his blame detector. If *you* don't supply the context for what you're saying, your partner will create one. The context he creates is likely to be less generous. He might see what you're saying as a form of nagging, anger, or a statement that he's not good enough. Such views are like a three-alarm fire, which inevitably leads to triggering your partner's blame detector.

The Operation

Once the positive intention is expressed, it's time to state how you'd like your partner to change. Again, your primary aim in conducting this delicate operation is to avoid triggering your mate's blame detector. The best way to do that is to take as much responsibility as possible for the problem at hand. For instance, let's say you want your partner to stop yelling at you when she's angry. If you say, "I want you to stop yelling at me when you're angry," her alarm and defense system is likely to be triggered. It implies that there is something wrong with her, and that only you know the right thing to do. Instead, you could take some responsibility for the problem by saying something like: "Ever since my mother used to yell at me as a little kid, I've been very afraid of people getting angry at me. When you raise your voice, it frightens me. I guess I'm really sensitive. I'd like to figure out a way we could be together without me being so afraid of having you raise your voice at me." By making yourself vulnerable—like in the preceding statement—and even taking responsibility for part of the problem, it will increase the chances of your partner being able to hear you without getting defensive.

Some people complain that such an approach sounds like you're walking on eggshells. Well, you are. The human ego is very fragile, and its defenses are very strong. In order to get past the ego's army of defenses, you have to have an impeccable communication plan. In fact, when it comes to requesting a change of behavior, it's a good idea to write down the exact words you want to say beforehand. That way, when the time comes to perform this delicate operation, there won't be any fatal errors.

From years of experience, I know how difficult it is to take responsibility for the problem you have with your partner. From your point of view, he is the cause of the problem, not the fact that you were abandoned by your father at age four. But again, place the responsibility on yourself. By doing this, you make it much more likely the other person will be willing to change. Fortunately, it's not necessary that you do this perfectly. If you've shown appreciation toward your partner and expressed your positive intention, he should be able to handle your feedback—even if you don't take full responsibility. If wording things just perfectly seems too difficult or weird for you, simply blurt out what's bothering you. Get it over with quickly. Then, do your best to move forward as quickly as possible.

If you've made it this far without triggering any alarms, you're ready for the most important step—getting your partner to agree to change. In my early days as a counselor, I used to immediately tell my clients how they needed to change in order to be happier. They rarely came back, and, even when they did, they almost never performed the actions I suggested. At first, I blamed them for "not really wanting to change." But then I realized I wasn't taking any responsibility for these "failures." Eventually, I realized most people don't want to be told how they need to change—even if they know you're right. Telling a person what she needs to do is a great way to lower her self-esteem. Instead, it's almost always best to ask her to come up with a new behavior to deal with the problem at hand.

In my counseling practice, I have found that practically all my clients can quickly solve their problems if, and this is a big if, I ask them the right question. We each have a storehouse of wisdom within us. Unfortunately, when we're in a defensive or annoyed state of mind, the doors to the wisdom vault are shut closed. Yet, when we're in a centered and loving state of mind, we can access this wisdom if we're asked a helpful question. If you've managed to avoid triggering your partner's blame detector, the right question will probably lead her to an immediately helpful solution.

What question is best to ask your partner to get her to change an annoying or destructive behavior? Here's the technique I've come up with: Say, "I need your help. I have difficulty with (express briefly what you'd like changed). How do you think we could do things differently in the future so we can better handle this situation?"

Your partner will have one of four responses: First, although it's unlikely, your partner still may get defensive. If that's the case, it's probably best to try this procedure again at a different time. Simply say, "I can see you're a bit upset right now. I'm sorry I brought it up at a bad time." A second possibility is that he'll make a suggestion that you think would actually work. When this occurs, shower him with praise. Say something like, "That's an *excellent* idea, honey! If you could do (whatever they suggested), I would so much appreciate it. Thank you for coming up with a solution that could really add to the intimacy in our relationship." Of course, use your own words—or your partner might feel patronized.

If your partner comes up with a truly bad solution or says, "I can't think of a solution," be careful how you proceed. What I've found works best is to say something like the following: "Would you be open to hearing some ideas I have for how we might better resolve this situation?" If they say no, then don't say anything more. Nothing can enter a closed mind. However, if you've made it this far without triggering any alarms, your mate will surely say yes. At this point, it's best to present at least a couple of solutions you've thought about. You might say, "My preference is that when you (briefly indicate the situation), that you (or we) could instead (briefly express the solution). If you'd be willing to try that, I'd be very grateful. But if that doesn't work for you, another idea is (express a second solution)." It's helpful to give your partner at least two possible solutions to choose from—even if you really prefer the first choice. When you offer just one idea, your partner might feel manipulated by you—and rebel against your solution. Yet, if you offer a few solutions, even ones you don't particularly prefer, it shows your partner you really are searching to solve the problem, rather than simply aiming to get your way at all costs.

Daniel came to me because his girlfriend, Anne, was always late for everything. It really bothered him, so he suggested to Anne they have a couples counseling session with me. Anne didn't want to go to counseling, so Daniel came to me looking for guidance for what he could do to better handle the problem at hand. After questioning him, I established that

Daniel really wanted Anne to change her ways, and he was looking for how to effectively make this happen. Previously, he had tried to bring up the subject, but Anne resisted. Immediately, she got defensive and didn't want to hear anything more. In my session with Daniel, using the ideas from this chapter, I coached him to say something like:

"Honey, I really appreciate how you are such a good cook. I feel really grateful when you take the time to make me a nice dinner like last night. You're a very giving person. So our connection can deepen even more, I'd like to talk to you about something that has been bothering me lately. I think if you and I can talk through this problem I'm having, we could have even more fun together. I've noticed I feel hurt and fearful when we arrive late to things together. Perhaps I feel insecure about what others will think, but whatever the reason it really makes me feel bad. I need your help. I'd like to make sure we arrive on time when we go places together. How do you think we could do things differently in the future so we can better handle this situation?"

When Daniel spoke these words to Anne, he was apprehensive about how she'd react. To his surprise, Anne was receptive. Instead of getting defensive, Anne made a couple of suggestions as to what would help her be ready on time. After a brief discussion, Daniel agreed to remind Anne when there were thirty minutes left before they had to leave the house. The plan worked. The feeling of having solved a nagging problem made both of them feel closer than ever before.

To help you remember this entire procedure, I've created an acronym: "A PI SWAP." The A stands for Appreciation. Remember to begin such encounters on a positive note. The PI stands for Positive Intention. Stating your positive intention creates a positive context for the feedback you'll be giving. The SW stands for the words Say What, as in say what you're having difficulty with. And finally, the AP is an abbreviation of the words Ask your Partner. Remember, it's almost always best to ask your partner how to improve the situation before suggesting what you think might help. When you feel it's important to provide your own suggestions, be sure to ask your partner's permission before you express your ideas. Simply ask, "Would you be open to hearing a couple of ideas I have that might work?" Such a question will help your partner feel respected instead of nagged and will assist him in being receptive to what you have to say.

Plan B

In the communication workshops I lead, I inevitably get this question: "What if my partner agrees to (whatever they've agreed to), and then they still don't do it?" A person who asks this question has usually employed the "nagging technique" of trying to get her partner to change. Her partner, in an attempt to have the nagging end, eventually gives in to the demands of his mate. But of course, since he didn't come up with the solution, he is unlikely to actually change his behavior in the future. If you use the "A PI SWAP" method, the chances are much better that your partner will follow through—because he came up with the solution. But, if your partner *still* exhibits the same old behavior, gently remind him of your agreement. In many cases, he may have simply forgotten—and will immediately follow through with the agreed upon solution. If he shows resistance to your reminder, or repeatedly forgets to do what was agreed upon, you need to be prepared with Plan B.

Plan B is a way of gently motivating your mate to stick to his agreements. In a nonjudgmental tone, report the facts of what has happened regarding the issue at hand. Then, say to your partner, "Even though you kindly agreed to do (whatever he agreed to), it doesn't seem to be happening. *What do you think we could do differently to make sure it happens in the future?*" Once again, rather than suggesting your own solution, you are first asking your partner for his idea. If his answer to that question works for you, then great. However, I've seen that people who are asked this question often say something like, "Well, I won't forget to do it again." Don't settle for that. After all, he's already been reminded by you, but to no avail. If you've tried reminding him in the past and it hasn't worked, you need to make a *new* agreement with some "teeth" in it.

I suggest you avoid pointing out to your mate that he's already forgotten the agreement before. Such a statement would likely only lead to defensiveness. Instead say to him, "*If in the unlikely event you forget to do (whatever he's agreed to), what do you think would be a fair consequence?*" That's a powerful question. People are motivated to avoid consequences, and the truth is there are definite consequences to breaking one's agreements. If your partner comes up with a "punishment" for breaking his agreement that's agreeable with you, then you're set. But if he says there shouldn't be a consequence, or that he simply won't blow it again, you've got more work to do. Following, I've detailed how to successfully handle a partner who breaks his agreements.

You: If, in the unlikely event you forget to take out the garbage on Monday morning again, what do you think would be a fair consequence?

Partner: I won't forget next time.

You: I'm glad you're willing to do it, but since you've forgotten a couple of times before, what do you think is a fair consequence if you forget again?

Partner: I don't know. I'll just do it.

You: Would you be willing to take me out to a nice dinner at Rinaldo's if you forget again?

Partner: I don't see why I should have any consequence if I forget. Sometimes I just forget. What's the big deal?

You: I understand. We all can make mistakes. I don't want to make you feel bad. Yet, there are consequences for our behavior. If I don't clean up after the dog, you've said we'll have to get rid of him. Therefore, I've cleaned up after him. I know your intention is to take out the garbage, but in case you forget again, I think there should be some consequence. What do you think is fair?

Partner: Okay, I'll take you to Rinaldo's if I forget again.

In this example, although the partner was being difficult, a workable solution was still agreed upon. In general, you should make it known to your partner there is indeed a consequence when he repeatedly breaks an agreement. Normally, the consequence is increasing anger and resentment—which does nobody any good. Using the method outlined previously, you begin by asking your partner for a *specific immediate consequence*. If he doesn't come up with anything, you can make your own suggestions. Whatever you come up with is fine, yet it needs to be something that works for both you and your mate. I know one couple who agreed that if the husband forgets to mow the lawn twice a month, the wife simply pays a gardener to do it. Since the husband doesn't want to spend the extra money, the new agreement has helped the husband to never (in three years) forget.

A step-by-step description of riding a bike sounds complex. But, once you get the feel of riding a bike, all the details of balance, peddling, and steering fall into place. In the same way, getting your partner to change seems like a complex operation at first. Yet, once you have the right feel for it, it can flow smoothly and quickly.

Katie came to me for counseling because she was having a hard time with her husband, George. She didn't like that he drank a lot, and they frequently argued over whether or not his drinking was a problem. I coached Katie in the "A PI SWAP" method, and had her record the operation in case it didn't go well. I'm happy to say Katie did an outstanding job. Following is the transcript of how the conversation went:

Katie: Sweetheart, thank you for taking me to the movies the other night. I really appreciate when you take me places so we can share special time together. In order to help us share more special times together, I'd like to talk to you about a difficulty I'm experiencing. Is now a good time for you?

George: As good as any.

Katie: Well, as I said, I want to feel even closer to you, and I'm finding there's something in the way of me being able to do that. My intention is to feel less anxious and more accepting of you. I think that would really add to our relationship. But as you know, I get worried about how much you drink. Because my dad drank a lot, when you drink, I feel frightened.

George: I can't help it if your dad drank a lot. That's not my problem.

Katie: That's true, but I'd like to feel more peaceful about this. I guess I need your help. What could we do differently that might help us both handle this situation more effectively?

George: I don't know. You could just stop worrying about it.

Katie: If I could do that, believe me, I would. But it really scares me when you drink, and I don't want to feel afraid of you. I want to have a fun, loving time together. What else might help to make this situation more agreeable for both of us?

George: Well, we could come to some compromise as to how much and how often I can drink. If I agree to stay within some boundaries that are acceptable to you, then maybe you wouldn't worry so much.

Katie: I think that's a wonderful idea! What do you think would be a fair agreement about your drinking that would help me to feel better?

George: How about I won't have more than three beers or two glasses of wine in any given night, and I'll limit my drinking to three times a week.

Katie: I think that's fair. That would certainly help me to worry less.

Katie was pretty sure George wouldn't keep to this agreement for long but kept her mouth shut to see what would happen. As she suspected, George drank about three glasses of wine and a couple of beers while at a friend's party. She knew to avoid speaking to him while he was drunk but approached him the next day. Here's how it went:

Katie: Honey, did you notice how much you drank at the party last night?

George: Oh, I don't know. Why? Did I seem a little tipsy?

Katie: Do you remember what you agreed to so I wouldn't feel uncomfortable or worried?

George: (said with a sense of dread) Oh yeah. Honey, I'm sorry—that won't happen again.

Katie: I appreciate the apology, but what should we do if it does happen again? I need to know I can rely on you.

George: Oh honey, it just happened this one time. It won't happen again.

Katie: Well, I know you have good intentions, but in the unlikely event it does happen again during the next year, would you be willing to go to counseling together?

George: All right, all right. But it won't be a problem. You don't have to worry about it.

If you analyze what Katie did, she simply used the principles of "A PI SWAP." When George broke his agreement, she administered Plan B, asking him questions until he agreed to consequences for breaking his agreement again. When you master these methods for getting your partner to change, it will make a dramatic difference in your relationship. In a matter of minutes, you can solve situations that might take other couples years to work through. A true communication miracle!

Writing Your Way to Harmony

Since the "A PI SWAP" strategy is very specific, some people like to write it down in a letter to their partner. I have found a high percentage of people react much better to letters than to verbal feedback. They can read the letter at a time that's convenient for them, and they don't have to react immediately to the feedback. In addition, writing an "A PI SWAP" letter to your mate has the added advantage of allowing you to be very precise about the words you use.

A couple named Tim and Jan had an ongoing problem with Jan's breath. Every time Tim tried to bring up the subject, Jan would immediately get defensive and upset. Finally, following the format of "A PI SWAP," Tim wrote Jan a letter. Here's what he wrote:

"Honey, I've been feeling very grateful lately, and its largely because you're in my life. We have so much fun together. I treasure our connection. To keep our relationship strong, I'd like to discuss something I've been having a hard time with. My hope is that, as we work through this issue, it will lead to even more fun and closeness. As you know, I've never liked vegetables very much, especially broccoli. For some reason, I've never cared for its taste or smell. I'm finding that, since you eat a lot of broccoli and other vegetables—I'm sometimes sensitive to the smell of your breath. Do you think we could figure out a way to deal with this so I could feel more comfortable when we kiss? I really appreciate what you've tried in the past, such as brushing your teeth, but that seems to help for only a couple of minutes.

Might there be something else we could try? Take some time to think about it. If you don't come up with anything, I have a couple of ideas that might work. I'm sure we'll be able to resolve this challenge, because I love you and I'm not going to let a little thing like this get in the way of our beautiful relationship. I love you, Tim."

Prior to this letter, Jan had refused to try any sort of breath mints or breath sprays. Instead, she insisted he was being too demanding and "didn't really want to be close." Yet, after reading this letter, Jan suggested to Tim she could use breath mints or sprays before they kissed and cuddled. Of course, Tim congratulated her for coming up with such good suggestions—and the problem was resolved. The pen can be even mightier than broccoli breath.

Miracle Reminders

1. It is important to carefully prepare your partner for hearing a request that she change her behavior. It's best if you can systematically plan what is going to be said and try to say it at a good time.

2. The acronym "A PI SWAP" represents how to ask your partner to change. First, appreciate your partner. Then, state your positive intention for requesting this change. Third, say what you'd like to change in specific detail. And lastly, ask your

partner for her input by saying something like the following: "I need your help. I have difficulty with (express briefly what you'd like changed). How do you think we could do things differently in the future so we can better handle this situation?" If your partner doesn't come up with any acceptable ideas on her own, ask her if she'd be open to hearing your ideas.

3. You may prefer and/or find it more effective to write on paper the entire "A PI SWAP" procedure. When you write, it helps you to be more precise with your words, and it makes it more likely your partner will accept your request without becoming defensive.

Mastery Practice

What is a small thing your partner does that you would like to have changed? Perhaps he blows his nose at the dinner table, and it bothers you. Or perhaps she interrupts you when you're on the phone. Whatever it is, use the "A PI SWAP" method to request he or she make the change you desire.

Chapter Ten

Negotiating Your Way Past Any Problem

You're either part of the solution, or you're part of the problem.
—Eldridge Cleaver

Frank and Cindy had only one big problem in their twenty-five-year marriage. Unfortunately, because they never resolved how to handle the money issue, they were constantly bickering. Despite twenty-five years of heated discussions, they hadn't made much progress. Like most couples with a thorny issue, they were still trying to decide whose problem it was, and the mere fact they were still arguing about it made them even madder. Several times a week, when some event would trigger their money buttons, they would endlessly repeat why it was their partner's problem that was causing the difficulty: a pointless waste of time.

Many couples fall into the same trap as Frank and Cindy, because they never actually agree on how to solve any of their problems; the result is that they have to keep dealing with the old ones—as well as all the new ones that inevitably arise. Before they realize it, couples can feel buried by an avalanche of problems. The way to sidestep this trap is to learn how to solve problems—once and for all, no matter what the issue is. However, like other communication skills, there are effective and ineffective ways to negotiate agreements that resolve problems. Couples who master this skill find that lasting trust and love is created.

In Chapter Seven I discussed how different rules between partners can have a major impact on the harmony in a relationship. I encouraged partners to reveal their rules in as much detail as possible. As partner's express their rules, areas of disagreement quickly become apparent. For example, if the woman feels the man should pay for everything, and the man feels otherwise—there is a problem.

This chapter is near the end of the book for a reason. To negotiate successful agreements, it's helpful to know all the previous information presented. You need to know about avoiding blame, how to be heard, how to help your partner feel loved, and especially about "A PI SWAP" from the previous chapter. The "A PI SWAP" method is a great way to *begin* the process of looking for solutions to problems you have in your relationship. To refresh your memory, the A stands for appreciation. Take turns appreciating something about your partner. This helps to remind both of you that, despite a difficult issue, you still care for each other. The PI stands for positive intention. Express to your partner the *ultimate result* you hope to achieve from creating an agreement. The SW stands for say what, as in say what you see as the problem or issue. And, finally, the AP stands for ask partner, as in ask your partner what they think is an equitable way to solve the issue at hand.

When negotiating an agreement with your partner, I've found it helpful to ask a slightly different question than what you asked when you wanted her to change. Negotiation is the art of compromise, and before asking your mate for solutions, it's helpful to give her a context in which her solutions could fit. You can do this by saying, "Considering my needs and desires with this issue, what do you propose might satisfy both our needs?" This question will help guide your partner to think of solutions that are more likely to work for both of you.

There are two added steps to creating agreements. The first I call "Create an Experiment." When trying to solve a problem, what commonly gets in the way is the fear of committing to any long-term agreement. After all, how can one know if a solution is fair and workable until it has been practiced in real life for a while? To avoid this fear of commitment, I suggest couples agree to a solution as an experiment. If they try something and it clearly doesn't work for one or both partners, either of you can request a new agreement. Typically, I suggest couples try a solution for a couple of weeks before they discuss together how well it's working. Having an experimental attitude toward solving problems makes it much easier to create agreements.

The second added step for negotiating agreements is to clearly declare what solution you are going to try. When making a declaration, it is important to be clear and to create a simple ritual that connotes that a deal has been reached. You might simply state the experimental solution out loud and shake hands or perhaps write it down on paper and sign it. Whatever you and your mate do, make sure there is a sense of clarity and commitment to the new approach of handling the problem. With the added steps of creating experimental solutions and declaring your agreement, "A PI SWAP" becomes "A PI SWAPED." The E is for experiments, the D for declare.

To see how such an approach works in real life, I'll use a recent example from my own relationship. When something angers or upsets me, I tend to exaggerate how bad the situation is. Helena quickly tries to point out how I could remedy the problem—which just annoys me further. As you read through the transcript of how we worked through this problem, keep in mind the "A PI SWAPED" acronym as a general map of what is occurring.

Me: Honey, I really appreciate how you are willing to give me honest feedback on my writing. It makes me feel cared for.

Helena: Oh, good, I enjoy doing it.

Me: I'm wondering if I could talk to you about a problem I've been having with expressing anger.

Helena: Sure, sweetheart. (She really does talk like this.)

Me: Well, I don't like how I express anger around you. My hope is we can come to an agreement about a better way we both can deal with my anger. I think if we can do that, I would be able to get over being angry more quickly and spend more time being intimate with you.

Helena: That sounds great, honey.

Me: I've noticed when I get upset, you immediately try to fix what causes it, or you try to convince me it's not as bad a situation as I'm making it out to be. Both these responses seem to make me more annoyed.

Helena: Do they make you more annoyed because you don't feel I'm listening to you?

Me: I think they bother me because it's not what I emotionally want in that moment. Since I'm upset, I guess I'm not very rational at those times. Do you have a guess as to what would help me work through my upset more quickly?

Helena: Well, I could just be silent and listen to you.

Me: I think that would be better than what's happening but not ideal. Would you be open to hearing my suggestion?

Helena: Sure.

Me: I'm embarrassed to say it, but during times I'm upset, I think I want you to give me lots of empathy and agree with me about how bad it really is. I want my pain to be fully acknowledged. Would you be willing to do that as an experiment when I'm angry—and we'll see if it works?

Helena: Okay.

Me: It's a deal?

Helena: A deal (we shake hands).

Because human beings are not predictable, your partner may interrupt or veer from your "A PI SWAPED" script. You too may slip up and get offtrack. But your job is to always bring it back. As you proceed through the steps of the agreement process, you'll finally create an agreement that may very well eliminate an entire category of problems from your relationship. Rather than feel your relationship is burdened with heavy problems, as you create workable agreements you'll once again feel the lightness and joy you felt when you first got together.

Since the rules we've used in the past for relationships have broken down, it's more important than ever to negotiate agreements with one's partner. Of the dynamite dozen, I've found the one that causes the biggest problem for most couples is the issue of money. Who pays for what and when? Who controls the money? What if you're married and one person wants to buy a new car and the other doesn't think it's prudent? These are tough questions, yet if you can work out agreements about how to handle these important issues, you'll save yourselves years of pain and struggle.

I taught the "A PI SWAPED" method to Frank and Cindy, the couple I saw who always argued about money. Like any couple who has struggled with a single issue for many years, there was a lot of emotional charge around the subject. Negotiating even a temporary solution was like walking a tightrope while drunk. Both Cindy and Frank had a tendency to fall off the rope—and fall victim to the endless cycle of blame. My job was to "throw them a bigger rope," in the form of reminding them about the "A PI SWAPED." Here's the transcript of what happened:

Me: Since we've been talking about what you appreciate about each other, I think we can skip that step for now. Cindy, why don't you begin by expressing what your positive intention is in trying to better resolve the money issue?

Cindy: Frank, I want to feel less tension and more trust in our relationship. I want to feel more in control of my life. I don't want to deal with your nonstop suspicion that I'm going to waste a lot of money on—

Me: Time out. That last statement sounded a lot like blame. Now move onto the next step. Say what you see is the problem.

Cindy: The problem is Frank has a problem with money . . .

Me: Time out. The blame detectors are wailing. Instead of talking about Frank, talk about what you want that you're not getting.

Frank: She always does that; she's always blaming me for everything.

Me: I'm not the judge, and you two are not presenting a case to me. Your goal here is to focus on resolving a problem that has consistently damaged your relationship. Let's try to avoid scoring points against each other and instead focus on coming up with possible solutions that might just help.

Cindy: The problem is that I would like to spend money without fearing that Frank is going to question every purchase I make. I would like to know how much money we actually do have, and if we have enough—sometimes spend some on ourselves rather than always putting it into our savings.

Me: Frank, why don't you say what you think the problem is?

Frank: The problem is she simply doesn't trust me to handle and control the money.

Me: I hear alarms going off, Frank. Would you care to restate that in terms of what you need that you're not getting?

Frank: Well, I don't feel comfortable having Cindy spend as much money as she would like to spend. I want to feel like we have enough money for our retirement, and I worry that unless I have control of the money, we won't have enough to be comfortable when we retire.

Me: Congratulations! You've made it at least halfway. Now I want both of you to take turns asking the other this question: "Considering my needs and desires with this issue, what do you propose might satisfy both our needs?"

Frank: Based on what you know about my needs, do you have suggestions for what would help to resolve this issue?

Cindy: As a matter of fact, I do. How about you keep control of the money, but you give me $75 a week to spend on whatever I like other than essentials and groceries. Also, I'd like for you to go over with me how much we have in our savings account and mutual funds, and if it looks like we're doing okay, plan a nice vacation together this year. In exchange, I agree not to use any of the credit cards without your permission, and I won't write a check for over $100 without your permission.

Frank: $75 a week, that's way too much! What do you need that kind of money for? I'm not a money tree. I have to work—

Me: Time out. Frank, rather than placing blame or making accusations, why don't you come up with a counterproposal that would work for you, keeping in mind Cindy's needs and desires?

Frank: Well, I'd be willing to go over our savings and such, and if we both agree we have enough money, we could plan a vacation. And I like the idea about not using the credit card without my permission and not writing checks over $100. But $75 a week for little knickknacks is way too much. I'd be willing to give her $30 a week—that's $120 a month!

Cindy: What can you buy for $30 a week? That's like living in poverty! I don't see why—

Me: Time out. Cindy, would you be willing to try $50 a week, just for a month to see if it works for you?

Cindy: Well, it's not what I want, but I'd be willing to try it.

Me: Frank, would you be willing to give Cindy $50 a week as an experiment to see if it would work?

Frank: I don't think that's very reasonable, but I don't see any other good option. I guess I'll try it—but just for a month. I want to be able to renegotiate this if it's not working.

Me: Both of you have the right to renegotiate this in a month if you don't feel it's working. Is it a deal?

Frank and Cindy: It's a deal.

Are you getting the hang of it? As you can see from Frank and Cindy, you must be more committed to reaching a solution than blaming your partner. Unfortunately, there's a major obstacle to using the "A PI SWAPED" method to resolve problems: It's hard work. Not only that, when you finally reach a satisfactory agreement, it won't feel particularly good. It will more likely feel as if you've received only part of what you wanted. After all, compromise means you give a little and you receive a little. On the other hand, continuing to blame your partner almost always feels good. You don't have to give at all, and you can feel righteous and indignant. The problem is, blame ultimately leads nowhere. It feels good in the moment, but it's like a cancer on the long-term prospects of your relationship because you never resolve anything. While resolving problems is hard work in the moment, the long-term effects on the relationship are increased love and harmony. Like many worthwhile things in life, you have to do some work before you can enjoy the rewards.

The upshot of the deal Frank and Cindy made is that it worked beautifully. As often happens, when the month was over they both were happy with how their experimental solution turned out. With this single agreement, their marriage was totally transformed. While they used to argue about money three or four times a week, in a whole month they had only one heated debate about money—an issue that was not covered in the agreement. Once they saw how well "A PI SWAPED" could work to resolve issues, they put other problems through the process. Not all their experimental solutions worked perfectly the first time, so occasionally they had to negotiate new solutions. Yet, within a matter of minutes, problems that had gnawed at them for years were often resolved.

As in the example of Frank and Cindy, the key step in the "A PI SWAPED" process is asking your partner something like the following question: *"Considering my needs and desires with this issue, what do you propose might satisfy both our needs?"* When you ask that question, it forces your partner to think in a very practical and problem-solving manner.

Because it's such a powerful question, you may find your mate initially resists the question or falls back into blame. Ask again. Ask until he finally answers or says he has no suggestions. If he has no suggestions, ask him, "Would you be open to hearing a couple of ideas I have?" One way or another, you want to steer the conversation toward practical, workable compromises.

Which issue in your relationship should you try to resolve first? My suggestion is to start off with a couple of little problems. This will help you to master the process before you tackle the really big issues. Once you feel comfortable with the process, feel free to slash your way through the dynamite dozen—or any other problem you currently are up against. With practice, you'll be amazed at how quickly you can create solutions for issues that have plagued you for years. While the solutions probably won't feel great at the moment, their long-term effects on your relationship will be miraculous.

Miracle Reminders

1. Most couples have to keep dealing with the same old problems, because they never come to a specific agreement as to how to resolve anything. To avoid this mess, learn to negotiate agreements that work for both partners.

2. To resolve a problem with your partner, begin with the "A PI SWAP" method. Then, remember to add two additional steps: Brainstorm experimental solutions you'd be willing to try, and once you agree on something, declare it as a done deal.

3. Keep the conversation focused toward searching for solutions by asking, "Considering my needs and desires with this issue, what do you propose might satisfy both our needs?" Keep negotiating back and forth with your partner until you both agree on a compromise solution.

Mastery Practice

Pick a problem you have with your partner and decide to negotiate a solution to it using the "A PI SWAPED" method. It could be an area where you have different rules and you want to avoid future problems, or it could be a current concern. It need not be a big problem. The important thing is for you to immediately practice and get a feel for the technique by using it with your partner.

Chapter Eleven

Repairing Broken Trust

He who excuses himself, accuses himself.
—Gabriel Meurier

Trust is like the foundation of a relationship. Without it, the whole structure of a relationship simply falls apart. Even if you communicate with great skill, but trust has been broken, you won't get anywhere. Your partner will simply see your attempts as insincere and not hear anything you say. Previously, I discussed how the triggering of your partner's blame detector can temporarily lead to her not being able to hear you. Yet, when trust is broken, your partner won't be able to ever hear you—until trust is repaired. In my counseling practice, I often see couples who have been hurt so many times by one another that all trust has been destroyed. Teaching them how to communicate better is necessary but not quite enough to repair the damage. Therefore, if trust is broken with your partner, you'll need to know some additional skills in order to handle it properly.

The first thing to do when you think your partner is pulling away is to find out if there's really a problem going on. I encourage clients to use what I call a "trust thermometer." A "ten" on the trust thermometer means your partner feels completely safe and trusting of you. A "one" on this scale means your mate doesn't trust you at all, and a "five" is about average. If you think your partner is pulling away, you can ask him or her, "Where am I on your trust thermometer scale?" If your mate says you're at six or more, you're probably doing okay, but if you're in the lower end of the scale, then there's some repair work that needs to take place.

Before discussing how to repair trust, it's useful to understand how it gets broken. There are two primary ways to damage or destroy the trust in a relationship. First, you can break an agreement with your partner. If the agreement is important enough, it may take only one broken promise to destroy the trust you've built together. For example, when one partner has an extramarital affair, it can often leave a relationship in shatters. The second way to damage trust is through hurting one's partner in various ways. As with broken promises, sometimes a single hurt can decimate trust—such as when a man physically abuses his partner. Yet, more frequently there's a pile of little hurts that finally breaks the camel's back. I counsel couples to handle broken promises and piles of hurts in slightly different ways. First, we'll talk about handling broken promises.

Broken Promises

Think back to a time when your mate broke an agreement with you, and you both knew it was his fault. What did you want from him? If you're like most people, you didn't want to hear his excuses and rationalizations. As his excuses babbled out, you probably became even more upset. When agreements are broken, I think people really need their partner to go through a four step process I abbreviate through the acronym "RARE." The R stands for responsibility. Before anything else occurs, if you break a promise, take responsibility for what you did. Only after you do that will your partner's ears be open to hear anything else. Taking responsibility means you now have an ability to respond to what's happened (response-ability). You can only respond if you first admit an agreement was broken.

After taking responsibility, apologize. People want to hear a sincere and heartfelt apology when they've been hurt. There's no getting around it. If you insist on avoiding this step, you'll end up hitting a wall. A sincere apology can go a long way in repairing trust. Since few people are willing to do it, it makes it even more powerful. Apologize for both the broken promise and the hurt that it caused. It won't cost you anything, and yet it will make a world of difference. In your partner's eyes, your stature as a person will dramatically rise.

The next letter is another R, which stands for request information. Ask your partner questions such as, "Is there anything I can do to help you feel better?" or "Is there anything you want from me right now?" People react to broken agreements in different ways. By asking your partner what she needs from you, it'll help her to know you truly care. Listen carefully to her response, and do what you can to satisfy any request she has of you.

Last, but not least in the RARE formula is E for entrust. The dictionary defines entrust as "to commit to another with confidence." When agreements and trust are broken, the final step in the healing process is to create a new agreement you're willing to keep. If you fail to do this, your mate will likely feel you're not sincerely sorry you broke their trust. But when you proclaim a new promise, it makes a statement to yourself and to your partner that you really want to change.

We all make mistakes. Yet, most people magnify their mistakes by blaming others or denying the fact they even made them. Don't go that route; it doesn't work. Instead, be a RARE person who accepts responsibility, apologizes, requests information to help the situation, and entrusts a new agreement they plan to keep. While this process may be difficult, it doesn't take long, and it's very effective.

A year ago, I made an explicit agreement with Helena to not talk on the phone on

Saturday nights—unless it was an emergency. Saturday nights are one of two nights a week where we make sure we spend quality time together. About a month ago, my sister called on Saturday night, and thinking it might be an emergency, I picked up the phone. It ended up it was just a social call, but I spent over an hour on the phone with her. By the time I got off the phone, Helena was quite upset. I had broken our agreement. My first impulse was to make excuses as to why it happened or to argue that it shouldn't be such a big deal. That would have added insult to injury. Instead, I used the RARE formula:

Me: I know you're upset, and you have every right to be angry because I broke one of our agreements. Honey, I'm really sorry I broke our agreement. I'm also sorry you're feeling hurt because of what I did. I made a mistake to answer the phone, but I didn't realize it until it was too late. Now that I've screwed up the evening, is there anything I can do to show you I care and help you to feel better?

Helena: (still upset) Why'd you answer the phone? You know how that makes me feel.

Me: I first thought it might be an emergency, and, by the time I realized it wasn't, I was unconsciously sucked into the conversation. I should have told her I needed to talk to her at another time, but I blew it. I'm really sorry. Is there anything I can do?

Helena: (still upset) You were on the phone for over an hour!

Me: You're right, and you have every reason to be mad at me. I totally ignored our agreement. I recommit to not answering the phone on Saturday nights, unless it's an emergency. Will you accept my apology and my renewed promise?

Helena: Okay. Can we hug? (We hug.)

In this example, I had to apologize and take responsibility a couple of times to satisfy Helena's need to know I was sincere. This is quite common. By taking the "one-down" position, and repeatedly admitting I was wrong, it helped her to once again trust me. In a two-minute conversation, Helena went from being very hurt and thinking I couldn't be trusted, to wanting to be close to me again. If that's not a magic, then nothing is.

A Pile of Hurts

When partners frequently violate their mate's rules, the hurts can pile up and finally break the trust in the relationship. Oftentimes, a seemingly insignificant thing will be the straw that breaks the camel's back. You may not even know that trust has been broken, because you may not have done anything obviously wrong. In such cases, it's hard to use the RARE formula, because you wouldn't know what to take responsibility for or why you're apologizing. Instead, when it seems like a small hurt has caused a major breach of trust, you need to have a different approach for repairing the damage.

If your partner is pulling away from you, it's a good idea to acknowledge her pain, even if you don't know why she's feeling bad. Avoid defending yourself, trying to immediately fix the situation, or turning away. Simply allow your partner to feel her feelings and have empathy for what she's experiencing. Such actions can go a long way in healing the hurt. You might ask her what she's feeling and compassionately tell her you're sorry she feels bad. Then, simply listen. See if you can gain a better understanding of what's going on. The more you understand what's going on in her head, the easier it will be to mend the broken trust she feels in her heart.

The next thing you need to know is exactly why your partner is pulling away from you. If you have not done something obviously wrong, and yet your partner is quite upset, she must have interpreted some behavior or event differently than you. Let me give an example. A few years ago, Helena and I were on one of our first vacations together. Unknowingly, in an effort to save money I was violating many of her rules, such as where we should stay on vacation, where we should eat, and so on. As it began to rain, we stopped at a supermarket to buy some groceries. I commented to her, "Don't get your down jacket wet or it'll be useless." As we drove away from the supermarket, I could tell Helena had completely shut down. The hurts had piled up and broken our fragile trust. I didn't know what I had done, but something was clearly wrong. Through acknowledging her pain and asking her gently probing questions, I found out my statement, "Don't get your down jacket wet or it'll be useless," had triggered her shutting down.

The rational side of me wanted to scream, "What's the big deal with saying that?" Luckily, I knew better. Obviously, Helena had made my statement mean something other than what I thought it meant. So I asked her, "What did you think I meant by making that comment about your jacket?" To make a long story short, she thought it meant I was putting her down for needing a lot of comfort, and that we probably couldn't be a couple because we were too different. Once I knew how she had interpreted what I said, I could effectively go about repairing our broken trust.

I have found the question, "What did you think I meant by that?" to be profoundly useful in clearing up misunderstandings and hurts. We naturally assume people react to words the same way we do, but that's clearly not the case. Only when we know what's really going on in our partner's head can we mend the hurts that pile up from misunderstandings. The more information we have, and the more accurate it is, the easier it is to repair the damage.

Hurts pile up in a relationship largely due to misunderstandings. Rather than tell Helena she was crazy to interpret my statement the way she did, I simply acknowledged how she had a right to feel hurt *based on the way she interpreted my statement.* Then I told her, "What I meant to say was I'm concerned about your health and comfort, and I know if your jacket gets wet, it won't keep you warm and comfortable anymore." When Helena saw the possibility I had a positive intention to my statement about her jacket, she no longer felt hurt. By clarifying the meaning of my words, the hurt could be repaired before it hemorrhaged into broken trust.

Once misunderstandings have been cleared up or talked about, the last step is to let your partner know how much you care. When people feel hurt, what hurts is the thought they are being rejected in some way. When Helena was hurt by my jacket statement, she was afraid I might not tolerate her need for comfort. The obvious antidote to her hurt was to express my love for her. As soon as she was convinced I really loved her, our trust was restored. For a little misunderstanding like this, it didn't take long to convince her I loved and accepted her. If misunderstandings and hurts have gone unrepaired for a long time, it can be quite a task to convince your partner of your love. Knowing how to charm your partner's heart is helpful, and so is patience.

Frequently, I encounter couples who have recently suffered a big breach of trust, such as an affair, and those who have piled up so many hurts that only a major act of forgiveness will allow the relationship to move forward. When a partner has been very badly hurt, he will usually need to fully express his hurt and anger before he can really forgive his partner. This is often best done within the context of individual therapy. If the hurt partner tries to directly express his anger and hurt at his mate, it will frequently turn into an argument. Yet, in individual therapy you can get all those bad feelings out without doing additional harm.

When a client comes to me with a lot of pent up anger, sometimes I give him the task of writing a really angry letter to his partner. In this letter, he writes all the details of how and why he's angry. I tell him to make the letter as nasty and as specific as possible. At the end of the letter, I encourage him to write about why it is now beneficial to let go of all this anger. Then, once the letter is done, I have him burn it. The burning of the letter is a symbol—it's time to start anew. From a clean slate it's easier to rebuild trust.

Trust, like love, can't be smelled, touched, or tasted, and yet it has massive power. Although it is invisible to our eyes, it is evident in our hearts. It is important to make consistent efforts to keep the trust thermometer glowing warmly in your relationship—and to be aware when it starts to chill. The moment you notice trust has been damaged, work to repair it as soon as possible. Like a recent wound, broken trust can get infected and spread if the right aid is not quickly applied. Yet, just as bones can grow stronger as they heal from being broken, so can trust grow stronger from being properly repaired.

Miracle Reminders

1. Trust is the foundation of a relationship. It's helpful to be aware of how well (on a scale of one to ten) your partner trusts you, and you trust your partner. Always work to keep your trust strong, because once it's destroyed, it's hard to repair.

2. Trust can be broken by breaking important agreements with your partner. When that happens, restore trust by taking responsibility for what you did, apologize, request information on what your partner needs from you, and entrust a new commitment with your partner ("RARE").

3. Trust can also be damaged by repeatedly hurting your partner in small ways. To deal with this, check your partner's trust thermometer, acknowledge their feelings, clear up misunderstandings by asking "What did you think I meant by that?" and tell and show your mate how much he means to you.

Mastery Practice

At some time in the future, your partner will feel hurt or distant from you for some reason. If you suspect that's the case, ask him, "On a one to ten scale, where am I on the trust thermometer?" If you're at the lower end of the scale, use the RARE formula offered in this chapter, or clarify what's wrong by asking, "What did you think I meant by (whatever seemed to lead to the situation at hand)?" Once you've talked things over, ask for his trust thermometer number again, and see if the level of trust has gone up.

Chapter Twelve

Keeping Love Alive Long Term

Everybody is bound to bear patiently the results of their own example.
—Phaedrus

In order to keep love alive long term in your relationship, I recommend three simple practices. First, periodically do special things for your partner. Although this idea is just plain common sense, it is not common practice. With all the things we have to do in modern day life, practicing acts of kindness can get squeezed out of our busy schedule. My personal rule is to do at least one special thing for my sweetheart each week. Since I get caught up as much as the next guy, I ask myself each Sunday night, "What special thing could I do for my sweetie this week?" Then, I schedule it in my weekly planner.

When I tell seminar participants I schedule nice things for my partner, people wince.

Yes, it would be more romantic if they just happened—and sometimes they do. But some things are too important to leave to chance. By scheduling acts of kindness, I know I won't get too busy and accidentally neglect our relationship. What things do I schedule? It's the simple things, done consistently, that count the most. Things such as leaving a love note, buying flowers, giving her a shoulder massage. By discovering how to enchant her heart, I know that what I do will have a powerful effect. Such weekly deposits into our shared love account have added immensely to our relationship.

The second practice that leads to long-term love is the ability to communicate in a loving and effective manner. My hope is you will continue to practice, play with, and explore the full menu of methods offered in this book. As you see fit, feel free to adapt these techniques to meet your needs. These methods are like power tools to help you build the temple of love you've always wanted. Take care of these tools. Learn when, where, and how to use them properly. And always remember their ultimate purpose is to move you and your partner to deeper levels of love, harmony, and understanding.

Housecleaning

A third and final prescription for maintaining a loving relationship is what I call weekly housecleaning. Since no one likes to talk about difficult things, we often put them off. Of course, this simply allows them to build up and eventually turn into big, hairy monsters. Housecleaning is a time set aside each week to clean up any resentments or problems that have accumulated in the relationship. During this time, couples work to bring down any walls that are blocking the flow of love. In this book, I have presented many techniques for removing the barriers to love. Choose whatever you feel would work best for you and your partner. The important thing is to set aside a specific time each week to talk through whatever may have piled up. Once the discussion is over, end the talk by saying something you love or appreciate about your partner. This weekly cleaning ritual can make a world of difference.

As you get better at using the ideas and methods in this book, you should have little or nothing to clean up at the end of the week. It's usually best to clean up messes right when they happen. Yet, people often forget to do that, so the ritual of a weekly time to clear up resentments or hurts is useful. Following is a series of questions you can answer with your partner that will help you to quickly clear up blocks to intimacy. If you don't have time to go through the entire list of questions, there's one question that quickly gets to the heart of the matter: *"Is there anything you're avoiding saying or communicating to me? If so, what is it?"* When you get asked this question and you become aware of something, you will probably want to avoid talking about it. Instead, be courageous. Make a commitment to be honest in your relationship. Don't settle for a relationship mired by petty resentments and unexpressed hurts or desires.

The questions that follow are designed to help you and your partner share important information, which may not have been talked about during the course of a busy week. Take as long as you like to answer each question. Once you're done, *ask the same question* of your partner. When you're the one asking the question, feel free to ask your mate related questions that might further clarify or expand upon his or her initial response. If a brief conversation naturally unfolds, that's perfectly all right as well. Although I suggest answering these questions once a week with your partner, you're welcome to use them in other ways. Many couples have told me these questions help stimulate intimate conversations when they are having a nice dinner together or driving on a long trip. Feel free to adapt them to meet your needs. If possible, create enough time and an environment free of distractions so you can better enjoy this process and experience deeper intimacy with your mate. Good luck:

1. What was the best thing that happened to you this past week?

2. When did you feel closest to me this past week? Why?

3. When did you feel most distant from me this past week? Why?

4. What are you excited about or looking forward to doing in the near future?

5. What are you concerned about or worried about?

6. What have you recently felt grateful for? Why?

7. Is there anything you're avoiding saying or communicating to me? If so, what is it?

8. What have you appreciated about me this past week?

9. What have you appreciated about yourself this past week?

Final Advice

In my counseling practice, I've been honored to witness the transformation that happens when people learn how to communicate effectively. The good news is that being able to communicate in a loving manner is a skill that can be learned. I don't think there is any other skill that could be so easily learned and have such a major impact on the quality of your day-to-day life.

There are a lot of ideas and methods in this book to practice, but perhaps a simple metaphor will help you remember the right spirit in which to use these tools. Think of a young, fragile, innocent baby. A good parent treats their baby with love, tenderness, and gentleness—for they know their baby is very vulnerable. Your partner and, indeed, you are like that baby. Although we hide our vulnerability and fear in a thousand different ways, underneath our masks we are still very sensitive and easily hurt. The more your partner protects himself through lying, hiding, or blame, the more hurt and afraid he is. In your mind, see his vulnerability. Treat him as you would an innocent child, with love and tenderness. By creating a safe space for him to be the innocent child he is, the love between the two of you will grow.

You may encounter difficulties along your path of love that feel like a momentous wall. If that's the case, don't hesitate to get professional help. An effective psychotherapist can help make sense of the chaos and confusion you may find yourself in. Several years ago when Helena and I were going through a difficult period, we went to a therapist for a few sessions. Even though I knew all the right techniques, I knew we were stuck. It was definitely humbling to be a therapist and yet pay to see a therapist for help in my own relationship. Yet, it was one of the best things we ever did. The therapist quickly helped us past the impasse we had hit, and once over the wall, our communication skills have kept the love flowing ever since.

A few years ago, I had a dramatic encounter that helped me learn the importance of love, communication, and intimate relationships. I was being driven in a van with eight other people to the local airport. At seventy-five miles per hour, we hit a patch of ice and the van skidded sideways, overturned several times, and finally screeched to a halt. While this event was happening, my whole life passed before my eyes. I knew I might be dead soon, but I was peaceful. I began evaluating my life based on how loving I'd been and how well I had expressed that love. Fortunately, I walked away from that accident relatively unharmed. In the ensuing years, I've talked to many other people who have had near death experiences, and they've all reported similar stories. Perhaps the main reason we are given the gift of life is to learn about love. Intimate relationships are a wonderful school for learning how to love more purely and effectively. Each and every step we take on the road toward love is a holy act. I wish you many blessings on your sacred journey.

Chapter Thirteen

Exercises for Communication Mastery

The following exercises were presented at the end of each chapter in the book. I have listed all of them here for your convenience. If you have not yet completed them, I urge you to do so now. The only way to master these methods is through practice:

1. Try acknowledging and appreciating your partner this week. Validate his feelings and tell him how much you appreciate specific things he does. Notice what effect this has on him and on your relationship.

2. If you haven't already done so, find out what helps to charm your partner's heart. The shorthand way of doing this is by asking your partner, "When are a couple of times you've felt most loved by me?" Pause for her answer, then proceed. "What helped you know

during those occasions that I really loved you?" For a more thorough explanation of how to find out what makes your partner feel loved, reread Chapter Two. Also, tell your partner what she does that helps you feel fully loved by her.

3. During the next few days, focus on using nonverbal methods to increase feelings of intimacy with your partner. Try smiling, mirroring your partner's body position, touching him frequently, and/or using the electric sex technique. Pick one of these methods right now and vow to use it tonight with your partner.

4. The next time you notice you're slightly upset at your partner, ask yourself the three questions abbreviated in the acronym WILL WISE: "What is likely to happen if I continue to insist on being right? Would I like to feel loved or be right? What is something I especially like about my partner?" Notice if thoroughly answering these three questions to yourself helps you to avoid blame and communicate in a more loving manner.

5. The next time you begin having an argument with your partner, immediately ask him to do a Spoon Tune with you. See how differently you feel after four or five minutes of tuning with him. Or if you prefer, you can do the "And What Else?" game instead. *Right now,* make an agreement with your partner to do one of these tools the next time either of you request

it. You might even create a negative consequence if the tool isn't immediately tried when requested. It's a good idea to put this agreement in writing.

6. Think of something that feels off or bad in your relationship that you haven't communicated to your partner. Communicate about it to your partner by using the following formula: "When you (briefly describe the situaution) I feel (sad, impatient, hurt, and/or fearful) because I (explain the psychological need you have that leads you to feel this way). What I want is (state your specific desire)." See if you can avoid triggering your partner's blame detector as you communicate your feelings and desires.

7. What is a problem area that repeatedly comes up in your relationship? If nothing comes to mind, look through the dynamite dozen (in Chapter Seven) and choose one area that has given you and your partner trouble in the past. Ask yourself and your partner the following question: "What does it take or what has to happen in order for me (or you) to feel good about (name the area you're exploring)?" Attempt to clarify your own and your partner's *specific* expectations in this area.

8. Using the information from Chapter Eight, see if you can create a metaphor that helps your partner understand how you feel about something in your life or relationship. Once you've created it, tell her and see if she seems to better understand you.

9. What is a small thing your partner does that you would like him to change? Perhaps he blows his nose at the dinner table, and it bothers you. Or perhaps she interrupts you when you're on the phone. Whatever it is, use the "A PI SWAP" method to request that he or she make the change you desire.

10. Pick a small problem you have with your partner and decide to negotiate a solution to it using the "A PI SWAPED" method from Chapter Ten. It need not be a big problem. It can even be insignificant. The important thing is for you to practice and get a feel for the technique by using it with your sweetheart.

11. At some time in the future, your partner will feel hurt or distant from you for some reason. If you suspect that's the case, ask her "Where am I on your trust thermometer?" Request that she give you a number from one to ten. If you're at the lower end of the scale due to breaking an agreement, use the RARE formula by taking responsibility, apologizing, requesting information on what your partner needs from you, and entrusting a new promise. If you don't know why she feels hurt, clarify what's wrong by asking her, "What did you think I meant by . . . ?" Once you've talked things over, ask for her trust thermometer number again, and see if the level of trust has gone up.

12. Do something special for your partner—for no particular reason other than as a loving surprise. You might write him a caring note, buy him a gift he would like, or offer him anything else you think would make him feel loved and appreciated. Notice what effect this giving gesture has on your relationship.

Chapter Fourteen

Reminder Cards

Throughout this book, I've used acronyms and catchy names of techniques to help remind you of the various methods I've suggested. Many of my clients have found it helpful to have these acronyms and methods on flashcards, so they can more easily remember to use them. In fact, some clients have even taped these flashcards in key locations throughout their house! When a heated discussion begins, they catch a glimpse of the flashcard and are immediately reminded of a more effective way to communicate with their partner. I encourage you to cut out these cards and use them as a helpful reminder.

WILL WISE
1. What is likely to happen if I insist on being right?
2. Would I like to feel loved or be right?
3. What is something I especially like about my partner?

Acknowledge your partner's experience and feelings.
Appreciate him or her.
Accept him or her just as as he or she is.

Spoon Tune if feeling stressed or separate or use . . .
And What Else?

When you . . . , I feel (sad, impatient, hurt, and/or fearful) because I (explain why). What I want is (be very specific).

A PI SWAPED
1. Appreciate your partner
2. Say your Positive Intention
3. Say What you see as the problem or what you'd like him or her to change
4. Ask Partner for input and solutions
5. Negotiate an Experimental solution
6. Declare your agreement

RARE
Take Responsibility for what you did.
Apologize for wrong doings.
Request info on your partner's needs.
Entrust a new promise to your partner.

Acknowledgments

This book wouldn't have come about without the ideas and encouragement of Mary Jane Ryan at Conari Press. Thanks again—you're always great to work with.

I also want to thank the following people for their contribution to my life and to this book:

To my partner of many wonderful years, Helena, for her nonstop love, support, and ability to create a safe atmosphere in which I could fully express myself. I love you, sweetie.

To my former girlfriends Mari, Jem, Cindy, Su, and Carol for putting up with me when I was not very skillful at communicating, and lovingly helping me discover what works.

To Joel Rosenberg, Justin Gold, and Marshall Rosenberg who have showed me through their instruction and their character how to communicate in heartfelt ways.

To my Uncle Lew for inspiring me with his hypnotic charm to explore
the far reaches of my mind and beyond.

To my brother Gary for always being there to help me with my books.

To my four parents for their support, encouragement, feedback, and love.

To my dog, Rama, for showing me how easily and powerfully love can be expressed.

And lastly, to the people I've seen in therapy and in my communication workshops,
who have tried my methods and shared with me their stories, feedback, and successes.
I thank each of you for your commitment to deeper intimacy.

About the Author

Jonathan Robinson is a psychotherapist, author, and professional speaker from Santa Barbara, California. Mr. Robinson is known for providing people with practical tools they can immediately use to enhance their life. He has appeared on "Oprah," CNN, and many other TV talk shows, and his work has been featured in *USA TODAY, New Age Journal,* and *Newsweek* magazines. Jonathan teaches workshops and speaks to corporations, associations, and churches around the country in the areas of practical spirituality, communication, and peak performance skills. He is the author of three other books, including the best-selling *The Little Book of Big Questions.* For free information about Mr. Robinson's talks and workshops, or a free catalog of his various audio and videotapes, write to:

Jonathan Robinson
P.O. Box 1501
Santa Barbara, CA 93102
Fax (805) 967-4128